DOCTORS' COMMONS AND THE OLD
COURT OF ADMIRALTY

DOCTORS' COMMONS AND THE OLD COURT OF ADMIRALTY:

A Short History of the Civilians in England

BY

WILLIAM SENIOR

OF THE MIDDLE TEMPLE, BARRISTER-AT-LAW

LONGMANS, GREEN AND CO.
39 PATERNOSTER ROW, LONDON, E.C. 4
NEW YORK, TORONTO
BOMBAY, CALCUTTA AND MADRAS
1922

PREFACE

WHEN a Doctor of Law, duly armed with the rescript of the Archbishop of Canterbury's Vicar-general, sought admission to the College of Advocates at Doctors' Commons, his ceremonial introduction took place first in the Court of Arches before the Dean, and only afterwards in the Court of Admiralty before the Judge—assuming, as was not always the case, that the two offices were filled by different persons. In the following pages the precedence thus formally given to the ecclesiastical side of Doctors' Commons has been purposely disregarded. In the first place, the part played by the doctors in foreign affairs, and in the development of maritime law, a field in which the Civilians for a long time showed the common law the way, seems a topic of wider interest than anything they did as Canonists : and secondly, the consideration of the position of the Canon lawyer as to *jus commune ecclesiasticum* after the Reformation leads straight to the still troubled waters of the controversy whether the Church in England before that period was a national church or only two provinces of the super-national Catholic one. For these reasons, and because the story of a bygone profession needs but a little book, I have dwelt mainly upon the work of the doctors in the maritime courts and in the diplomatic service of the State.

W. S.

CONTENTS

I. ENGLAND AND THE CIVIL LAW

HERE and there in England are to be found small country churches which are miniature Roman basilicas in plan, and show other traces of an influence that must have travelled hither as far as from Ravenna, that last refuge of the rulers of the Western Empire, or even from the capital city of Justinian itself. To some minds such buildings have a romantic attraction that is lacking in others more purely indigenous. One must not push the parallel too far, but the Romanic traces in English legal institutions have for the historically inclined something of the same glamour. Both, at any rate, recall a singleness of culture that has long vanished from that part of the world which used to be called Christendom.

Much that awakens this kind of interest concerning the Romanic waves of jurisprudence that welled into Britain in early days has been said by the learned authors of " The History of English Law before the Time of Edward the First " ; but the whole story of the influence of the Corpus Iuris upon the growth of English law throughout its development has yet to be written. An account of the men who from time to time have professed the Roman Law in England, either as teachers or practitioners, even if it were much fuller than the following sketch can claim to be, would not, of course, tell that story, although it might here and there throw sidelights upon the more scientific

B

work. Apart from its influence, that is to say, as a separate system, the Roman Law in England came to nothing. We may perhaps claim for the doctors of the civil law in this country something of the interest that attaches itself to those who stand for lost causes. But once, if not twice, they came near to winning.

There is anyhow the interest of a contest. The historian of the fortunes of the Roman Law in England, when he appears, will first of all be concerned with showing " how the full development " of the national law, and the confidence felt in " its strength and capacity to stand alone, produced " an antagonism between it and the Roman Law, " which drove the latter from Westminster Hall : " how the Roman Law nevertheless gained ground " in the ecclesiastical courts, and in the Equity " system under praetor-chancellors : and finally " how, at length, the increase of social and com- " mercial intercourse and the absence of a finished " national law of obligations led to the Roman Law " being appealed to as a Ius Gentium, whose rich " materials might supply the deficiencies of the " younger law in such matters." [1]

It was, in fact, as the exponents of a common law of nations that the civilians as an organized profession obtained their footing ; and it will be with the civilian as an admiralty and international lawyer that we shall chiefly have to do. But the earlier centuries must be briefly glanced at, not

[1] Gütenbock, " Bracton and His Relation to the Roman Law." Coxe's trans., p. 14.

only because they show that the rôle into which he ultimately settled down was already being marked out for him, but also because they explain how he came to be confined to it.

The first formal teaching of the Roman Law in England by Master Vacarius was silenced by King Stephen about the year 1151. Not very effectually or permanently maybe ; but John of Salisbury, who chronicles Stephen's veto, does not omit to remind us that England was a country " *ubi inveterata consuetudo obtineat.*" On each occasion afterwards, when there seemed to be a probability of a substantial incursion of the Roman Law into this country the barrier of a home-grown system was strong enough to withstand it The Roman Law might be " divinely reasonable," but it was an outlandish thing.

The close of the thirteenth century, " the age that witnessed the greatest inroad of written law upon custom and tradition that had occurred since the date of the Capitularies," was the first of these occasions. It was at this time that Edward Plantagenet came to the throne of England, a ruler who, although his title of " the English Justinian " has no reference to the fact that Roman Law was then very much in the air, would perhaps have given it more aptness than it has if the temper of his people had permitted him. He was unquestionably a born law-giver, and the civilian lawyer was then ever in the train of kings. His father, Henry the Third, had retained in his pay Henry

of Segusio, the canonist, afterwards known as
Hostiensis, because he became Cardinal-bishop of
Ostia, but who seems to have been not merely a
canonist, but a doctor *utriusque iuris* of Bologna.
Edward's brother-in-law, Alfonzo the Wise of
Castile, was attempting to supersede the national
customs of his own kingdom by the scientific
jurisprudence of Rome : [1] and Edward himself
about the same time snatched away the younger
Accursius from his chair of civil law at Bologna to
be his councillor—much to the chagrin of the local
authorities, who valued their professor and seques-
trated his property by way of reprisal.   Franciscus
Accursius was a lesser light than his famous father,
the great glossator and pupil of Azo—*patre longe
obscurior*, as Freherus says—but he was doubtless
as accomplished a legist as Edward could lay hands
on.   This was in 1275, and Accursius was for
several years afterwards " *dilectus et fidelis secre-
tarius noster*."   Some examples of the kind of work
the King found for him may be given.   In the same
year he was appointed along with Master William
de Corneria, " professor of both laws," and other
persons, a King's proctor in the parliament and
courts of Philip of France in causes begun between
Henry the Third and Louis the late King of France.[2]
In the following year a commission was issued to
him and Nicholas de Stapleton empowering them
to inquire and do justice as to the plaint of the
Jews of Oxford that the Sheriff had lately com-

---

[1] Stubbs, " Const. Hist.," II. 199.
[2] Cal. Patent Rolls.   Ed. I.   June 8, 1275.

pelled them to pay " certain undue extortions ";[1] an appointment also of a quasi-international character, since Jewry was allowed laws and tribunals of its own. About 1278 he appears to have gone as envoy to the Court of Rome, since we find a mandate to certain merchants of Lucca to pay him and his fellows " their reasonable expenses in going, staying and returning thither."[2] There are circumstances in what we know of the employment of Accursius, attributable to Edward's want of pence, that seem like an augury of the precarious nature, very nearly throughout its length, of the civilian's professional existence in England. The annuity or yearly fee of forty marks that the King granted to the lawyer was at one time no less than five years in arrear. We have on record Edward's belated acknowledgement of indebtedness to the merchants of Pistoja, who had been trusting enough to pay these arrears to Accursius for him.[3] But, however the doctors might be treated by princes, the science they professed was in high repute. Just twenty years after Edward's accession comes the great lawsuit for the Crown of Scotland, in which he was not merely arbitrator but judge. The procedure on that occasion appears to have been closely copied from the old Roman Centumvirale Iudicium ;[4]

[1] Cal. Patent Rolls. Ed. I. May 18, 1276.
[2] Cal. Patent Rolls. Ed. I. Sept. 17, 1278.
[3] Cal. Patent Rolls. Ed. I. June 15, 1290.
[4] See " Brus *v.* Balliol, 1291–1292 : The Model for Edward I.'s Tribunal," by Geo. Neilson, LL.D., *Scottish Hist Rev.*, Vol. XVI., p. 1.

and amongst the names of the panel of auditors nominated by the King is that of William of Kylkenny, " iuris civilis professor."[1]   Edward still does not lack the services of civilians, although by this time Accursius has returned home, and early in the fourteenth century, Master Philip Martel, professor of civil law, becomes prominent amongst the King's clerks.   In 1304 this civilian is appointed along with the Constable of Dover Castle to go to Calais and there in conjunction with the two deputies named by the King of France to make inquisition touching depredations at sea committed by the men of Calais and of the Cinque Ports upon one another ; [2] William de Grenefeld, Canon of York and professor of the civil law, had already been sent by Edward to France to settle the terms of a treaty relative to disputes arising out of things done at sea.[3]   The line that would lead to the civilian of the seventeenth century, at once ambassador and Admiralty Court Judge, was already beginning to be traced.

But as yet, that is to say, up to the middle of the fourteenth century, it is the rôle of negotiator in foreign affairs that is his most prominent one. We shall in our next section endeavour to explain how, soon afterwards, he came to take his seat in the maritime courts.   Before leaving the earlier days of the civilians' employment in England, however, the name of John de Shordych should be

[1] Rymer : " Foedera," i. 766.
[2] Cal. Patent Rolls.   Ed. I.   Jan. 28, 1304.
[3] See Preface to " Year Books of Ed. I.   Years 30–31," p. xix.

mentioned, because he was an Englishman and, so far as appears, not an ecclesiastic—two facts that distinguish him from most of his compeers at this time, who were usually priests or foreigners or both. In 1329 he was appointed along with others to treat with Philip of France ;[1] and Adam Murimuth has left us an account of his interview with Pope Clement at Avignon in 1343, when sent with letters from the Parliament of England to protest against the holding of English benefices by foreign priests. Murimuth calls him " *miles sapiens et iuris professor,*" and after describing the meeting, which did not lack boldness on John's part, tells us that he hurried away to Bordeaux, " *alia negotia domini regis expediturus.*"[2]

But in spite of the constant presence of civilians at the elbow of the English Justinian, the bid of the Roman wisdom for any full and open kind of naturalisation came too late. The national law was already able to stand on its own feet. Since the time of Henry the Second the English customs had been in process of consolidation through the circuits of the itinerant justices. The " Year Books " begin in 1292, showing a plentiful crop of litigation in the courts administering the nascent common law. And yet although this development of a national law was going on, the century and a half which had preceded the death of Edward the First—that is to say, the period between the middle of the twelfth and the end of the thirteenth

[1] See Rymer, "Foedera." ii., *passim*.
[2] " Adami Murimuthensis Chronica," Hog., pp. 152, 3.

century, has been styled the Roman epoch of English legal history.[1] That is because it was the period of unacknowledged leavening. Though the title of the great work that Bracton had written about the middle of the thirteenth century is, as all the world knows, " De Legibus et Consuetudinibus Angliæ," we meet in it many maxims of the Roman Law which had already become proverbial and appear to be already naturalised in England ; [2] and not only maxims, for the whole of the doctrines relating to personal actions were based by Bracton upon the Institutes and the Digest.[3] There is no need to discuss Bracton or his book in this place : probably the statement quoted by Wynne [4] that he " was a Doctor of both laws before he came to our bench " means no more than that his reading, as is obvious, had comprised both Digest and Decretals. There does not appear to be any certainty of his academical status. As to his book, " Romanesque in form, English in substance," [5] based on English records, yet arranged after Roman models, its method enables us the better to under- stand the statement of Spelman that a " great portion of our Common Law is derived from the Civil Law " ; brought into it, he considers " by such of our Reverend Judges and Sages of ancient

---

[1] By Biener. Gütenbock, " Bracton and His Relation to the Roman Law," p. 17.

[2] Gütenbock, *ibid.*, p. 48.

[3] Spence, " The Equitable Jurisdiction of the Court of Chancery," Vol. I., p. 224, note.

[4] " Eunomus," Vol. I., p. 77.

[5] Pollock and Maitland, " Hist. of English Law," i. pp. 207-8. And see the whole chapter on " The Age of Bracton."

time as for Justice and Knowledge sake sought
instruction there, when they found no rule at home
to guide their judgments by."[1]   John de Lexington,
a justice in Eyre in 1251, is also *in utroque iure
Canonico scilicet et civili peritus*.   One effect of
the introduction of Roman elements through
the process the result of which is known as
judge-made law, would naturally be to take the
wind out of the sails of the out-and-out Romanisers:
and our present point is that books such as
Bracton's, romanesque and English at the same
time, also contributed to that end.   Whether he
shrewdly foresaw it or not, subsequent ages
accepted as English law, upon his authority, pass-
ages but slightly altered from the "Institutes" of
Justinian.[2]   The Roman Law was thus removed
from being regarded as an open competitor.   The
point, so far at least as it concerns form, was in
fact made by Abraham Fraunce, writing in the
sixteenth century, when the comparative merits
of the civil law and of the native system came again
to be canvassed.   In the plea for a greater *rapprochement* between scholarship and law which is
contained in his Preface to " The Lawyer's Logicke "
—a plea addressed " To the learned Lawyers of
England, especially the gentlemen of Gray's Inn "
—Fraunce avoids expressly deciding which system
is the better but adroitly points out that even if
the method of Justinian were as perfect " as some
" say it is, then I say we have our Common Lawe

---

[1] " Reliquiae." 1723 ed., p. 99.
[2] See the judgment of Holt, C. J., in Coggs *v.* Bernard.

" penned after the self-same methode two hundreth
" years agoe by that famous and learned Judge
" Henry de Bracton, skilful in both thease lawes." [1]

There were, moreover, in addition to the de-
veloping strength of the national law, two other
reasons why at the time of the first Edward the
tide of the Roman jurisprudence tended to be
pushed back. At the back of the imperial system
were maxims of kingly absolutism that even the
embryonic constitutional law of that day would not
listen to. Bracton in alluding to the Lex Regia
had felt constrained to water it down to the point
of misrepresentation. We shall hear again of the
maxim, *Quod principi placuit legis habet vigorem,*
and the colour it was supposed to give to the activities of the professors of the Roman law in the
political field. As to Edward the First, we are
told by the chronicler that when in 1299 he declined
to confirm the charters unless the words " *salvo iure
coronae nostrae* " were tacked on to them, he was
obliged to withdraw from his position, *consiliarii
regis timentes seditionem populi.*[2] The other subsidiary reason why the Roman jurisprudence did
not at this time make the headway that upon its
intrinsic merits might have been expected was the
jealousy of the Canonist. By the middle of the
thirteenth century the Roman Law had come
temporarily under the displeasure of the Church,
and it is to be remembered that the great majority
of lawyers were still at this date clerks in orders.

[1] *Op. cit.* Introduction.
[2] "Hemingford." Vol. II., p. 183.

The Church had perfected a vast legal system of her own, built, it is true, upon the model of the imperial code, but a system in which Caesar, needless to say, was not placed above the Bishop of Rome. At the date of which we speak the civilian stood between the two fires of the Constitution and the Church. It may be added that a little later, by the time of the third Edward, he had, in virtue of this very connexion between the Canon and the Civil Law to share the opprobrium Roman ecclesiastical pretensions had aroused in the English mind.

The second occasion when, for a short time, Roman Law came near to overwhelming the common law of the realm, happened during the second quarter of the sixteenth century. " The continuity of English legal history," says Maitland, " was seriously threatened." [1] Of that, however, in its place ; it is enough to say here that after a period, as it were, of arrested development, the common law revived in time to be again strong enough to withstand the innovators.

Yet the Roman Law came to occupy a small field of its own in England side by side with the common law, by usage and immemorial custom. The proceedings of the military court of the Constable and Marshal, and of the courts of the two Universities were always in the hands of civilians : and if such tribunals were far removed from the main stream of national business, the same can hardly be said of the courts of the admiral, when they

[1] " English Law and the Renaissance," p. 17.

were established. It was there, amongst domestic institutions, that the civil law had its chief and acknowledged incidence. " Forasmuch as " strangers are not acquainted with our laws," wrote the Council to the English Ambassador in France in the year 1550, " to show them favour, " the King's Highness's progenitors have thought " good to erect and set up a court of matters " chanced upon the seas or out of the realm : in " the which court process is made and justice is " ministered according to the law civil, the which " Court is called the Admiralty Court : where the " said strangers' causes are examined, whether the " controversy be between themselves or against " the King's subjects."

This was but the application to matters of private international law of the assistance which the Roman Law afforded to the statesman and the publicist in affairs strictly international. We have already noted how from very early times the civilian had employment in this latter sphere. For centuries the Roman civil law stood for the Law of Nations.[1] When, at the time of the Commonwealth, Dr. Robert Wiseman put forth a book that has been called the last formal plea on behalf of the civilian's profession, he grounded the whole of his argument for " The Excellency of the Civil Law " upon that aspect of it.

Such, then, were the provinces in which the civilian openly worked. If we pass by his influence

[1] " Celui qui écoute le langage du droit romain entend à vrai dire le langage de toutes les nations." Bynkershoek.

upon the infancy of the national common law, we may say that he appears first in the rôle of negotiator, sent abroad on behalf of the State. His acquaintance with foreign peoples and the universality of his science made it not unnatural that he should presently annex the Court of Admiralty, as in fact he did, not very long after its establishment. And since the later history of that Court is, to a considerable extent, one of a long and losing battle with the courts of common law for possession of the mercantile litigation of the kingdom, the civilian's province has not been so remote from our general legal history as it would have been had it included only an embryonic Foreign Office.

II. THE FIRST ADMIRALTY
JUDGES

It is a commonplace of English legal history that
the proceedings of the ancient Court of Admiralty
were regulated by the Civil Law : but the circumstances in which the civilians made their entry
into their maritime heritage have not been very
closely investigated. The first point to be considered may be put as follows. In the ecclesiastical courts, going back (let us say) to Lanfranc
of Pavia, the mingling of the Civil and the Canon
Law at most, if not quite at all times [1] had been,
as Selden says, " not unlike the union of snakes
twisted about Mercury's wand." The civilian
ecclesiastic, trained in Italian schools, had there a
long-established footing. But the courts of the
admirals, military officers, come rather suddenly
into existence in the middle of the fourteenth
century : suddenly, because fifty years before, in
1297 to be exact, Berwood J. had remarked to
counsel, " *De poer de admiralle dont vous parle
ne scavomes rienes*," and Sir Matthew Hale's comment on this dictum is that " it is not to be imagined
" that the Judges of the common law should not
" have known there was such an admirall juris-
" diction if it had been then in use." [2] Nevertheless it is well known that before the end of the

[1] *Supra*, p. 10.
[2] A Dissertation touching the Jurisdiction of the Common Law
and Courts of Admiralty. Cap. 10. Hargrave, M. S., 93.

fourteenth century the courts of the admirals were
beginning to exceed their jurisdiction, and were
duly reproved by two statutes of Richard the
Second in 1389 and 1391. The courts, however,
with which they meddled and whose business they
in time absorbed, did not administer the Civil Law,
although a remote and unclaimed Roman ancestry
may have belonged to some part of the matters with
which they dealt. Yet in the middle of the sixteenth century, as we have seen, it is stated that
" process is made and justice is ministered in the
Admiralty Court according to the law civil " :
and when Villandry, the French Envoy to Edward
the Sixth, said that the King his master wished
that an agreement were made between the ordinances of England and France in marine affairs,
he could be told " that our ordinances were nothing
but the Civil Law and certain very old additions
" of the Realm." Selden, in his turn, has amplified
" this answer. " In the Court of Admiralty," he
wrote, " what occurs under the Titles *Ad legem*
" *Rhodiam de iactu, de nautico foenore, de usuris*
" *nauticis, de exercitoria actione*, and other matters
" belonging to Marine Affairs, are usually handled
" according to the Justinian Law and expressly
" taken from the Code of that Emperor and from
" Interpreters upon it. But yet in such a manner
" that the Oleronian Laws likewise or the Marine
" Customs so called may, as is practised by other
" Nations, be blended with it and be allowed to

" have the greatest Authority there." [1] The passage is here quoted at length because, like the earlier one, it distinguishes the old marine customary law from the Roman element. The same distinction had been drawn earlier still in the fifteenth century when, as if the latter were considered novel, we find it laid down that the lieutenants or judges of the admiral shall " only mix the law civil with the law maritime where it may be equitable." [2] If wo are to consider the rather elementary twenty-five or twenty-six articles, of which the more ancient versions of " the Oleronian Laws " consist, as representing the bulk of the marine customary law it seems probable that there would often arise a need of something to fill up the gaps. The Roman law had been a " Promptuary," to use a word of Selden's, for the shapers of the common law in Bracton's day ; in the development of the law maritime it was not only prompter but openly played a part, though nominally the part might be but a subsidiary one. About what date, then, did " the Justinian Law " openly seat itself, so to speak, side by side with the old " Marine Customs " ?

The early history of the Admiralty Court is admittedly obscure. We do not know the year of its beginning. The best authority only tells us that its origin can be traced " with tolerable certainty " to between 1340 and 1357, and that it was instituted to deal with piracy or " spoil " claims

[1] The Dissertation of John Selden, annexed to Fleta, p. 220.
[2] Mitchell, " Early History of Law Merchant (1904)," p. 77.

made by and against foreign sovereigns.[1] Its
earlier records are lost, but when we get them about
the year 1530 the Court is already seised of suits
concerning freight, average, sales of ships, and
goods, and other mercantile matters, which then
form the larger part of its business.[2] It is enough
however, for our present purpose to know that
there were usually two or three admirals, each of
them with courts and deputies sitting therein,
from about the middle of the fourteenth century
until the first years of the next. Precisely when
the Court of Admiralty became one and indivisible
need not at present concern us. Both the re-
straining statutes of Richard, already mentioned,
speak of the admirals and their deputies in the
plural throughout. Coke says that of ancient time
there were several admirals because the wisdom
of those days would not trust one man with so
great a charge ; but the extent of England's coast-
line has also to be considered. At any rate, in
1406, there is still an Admiral of the North and
another Admiral of the West, and also mention of
a " sub-admiral from the Thames to the south and
west of England," who was, like the others, provided with a lieutenant or deputy and everything
handsome about him.[3]

It is with these lieutenants, holding " sessions
within divers places of this realm " and " encroach-

---

[1] Marsden, " Select Pleas in the Court of Admiralty." I.,
p. lxvii.

[2] Carter, " Hist. of English Legal Institutions," 4th ed. (1910),
p. 278.

[3] Cal. of Patent Rolls. July 23, 1406.

ing to them divers jurisdictions " [1] that we have
here to do.   They were the first Admiralty judges.
It is all very well for the " Black Book of the
Admiralty " to begin with the counsel of perfection
—" when one is made Admiral he must first
" ordaine and substitute for his lieutenants, de-
" puties, and other officers under him, some of the
" most loyall, wise, and discreete persons in the
" maritime law and auncient customes of the seas
" which hee can anywhere find, to the end that by
" the helpe of God and their good and just govern-
" ment the office may be executed to the honour
" and good of the realme."   Stubbs has noted
" the apocryphal character of all the early records
of the Admiralty." [2]   The first deputies appointed
by the Admirals of Edward the Third's reign appear
to have been soldiers, and as an example of their
good and just government let us take the complaint
of the men of Scarborough in 1376.   The burgesses
allege that by charters of the King's progenitors
and his own confirmation it had been granted to
them to improve the wastes within the town ; that
there was a waste called " Sandes," lying between
their town and the quay, which they and their
ancestors had for the most part built upon ; that
they held their market and fair on the remainder
and had " been accustomed to make executions of
" debts trespasses and other contracts there by the
" bailiffs and ministers of the town " ; and that
they were " now newly prevented " from making

---

[1] 13 Rich. II., st. I. c. 5, and 15 Rich. II., st. 2, c. 3.
[2] " Constitutional History," Vol. II., p. 289.

such executions by the admiral's lieutenants, who asserted that the waste should pertain to the King.[1] It is evident that Sandes was the spot where the Law Merchant and the Rolls of Oleron would be upon occasion appealed to ; and one does not see why the admiral's lieutenants should have tried to dispossess the burgesses of it unless they were anxious to suppress Scarborough's quay-side court altogether. In that case the instruction to encroach on the jurisdiction of the seaports was being bettered.

At the risk of going over ground already well known, a word or two must be said here about the local maritime courts administering a customary law to passing merchants and mariners which were being harassed by the admirals. They are thought with good reason to have been copies on a smaller scale of those Courts of the Sea which are known to have existed in the mercantile cities of the Mediterranean at the beginning of the twelfth century.[2] The date of their establishment in England must be considerably earlier than those ascribed to the written custumals of certain seaport boroughs, which in a few cases have been preserved, and which contain versions of that body of medieval maritime law known as the Rolls of Oleron. Such collections are the Domesday of Ipswich, which belongs to the early fourteenth century, but recites how a " false common clerk of the town " had carried off an older book going back to the reign

---

[1] Cal. Patent Rolls. May 13, 1376.
[2] Twiss, " Black Book of the Admiralty," Vol. II., p. ix.

of John, the " Oak Book " of Southampton, dating
from about 1300, and the " Liber Memorandorum "
and the " Liber Horn " in the Guildhall of London,
which are ascribed to the earlier years of Edward
the Third. When the Laws of Oleron first had
authority in English seaports is uncertain,[1] but
there is no doubt that they were the recognized
code in matters within their scope in the courts of
the boroughs long before those of the admirals
came into being. So much is clear, not only from
the antiquity of the manuscripts containing them
and compiled in English towns for convenience of
reference, but from a case of Pilk *v.* Venore before
the mayor and bailiffs of Bristol in 1351, in which
the authority of the " lex de Oleron " is assumed.
Both plaintiff and defendant pleaded it, saying
" *talis est* " ; and the judgment was certified to the
Chancellor as based upon the *lex et consuetudo de
Oleron.*[2] It is to be noted also that the seaport
courts were lay tribunals : the record of Pilk *v.*
Venore describes it as having been tried " *in plena
" curia coram maiore et ballivis et aliis probis
" hominibus villae et magistris et marinariis.*"

Now although Sir Travers Twiss finds in portions
of the consuetudinary law of the sea, as it has come
down to us in various collections of maritime
customs, the laws of Oleron amongst the number,
certain points of resemblance to provisions in the
Roman civil law,[3] we may be sure that the good men

---

[1] As to this, see certain speculations in an article by Miss
G. F. Ward, *Eng. Hist. Rev.*, July, 1918.

[2] Transcribed by Prynne, " Animadversions," 117.

[3] " Law of Nations " (1861 ed.) Vol. I., p. 244 *et seq.*

of the town who dispensed justice on the quays of Ipswich and Bristol in the fourteenth century were unconscious of any connexion with the Digest. They knew that the law they administered was not the common law of England, though recognized and allowed ; and they were acquainted with the pie-powder courts of the fairs administering the law merchant, which was not common law either. Fair-ground, market, and quayside were all one at Scarborough, as we have seen. The kinship between the law maritime and the law merchant, quaintly described by Malynes at a much later time—" even as the roundness of the Globe of " the world is composed of the Earth and Waters, " so the body of Lex Mercatoria is made and " framed of the Merchants' Customs and the Sea " Laws, which are involved together as the Seas " and the Earth " [1]—was a reality even when in the fourteenth century the bailiffs of Scarborough and Bristol dealt with them. But it followed that the law laid down by those worthies could not fail sometimes to be what would now be called private international law. Venore, the defendant in the Bristol case cited above, was a master-mariner of Bayonne. Fifty years earlier we find amongst the names of the suitors in the Fair Court of St. Ives those of merchants from Louvain, Rouen, St. Trond, Germany and Florence.[2]

Of the influence of the medieval fairs, continental and English, it has been said that " like the Church

[1] " Consuetudo et Lex Mercatoria " (1686). Preface.
[2] " Rolls of the Fair Court of St. Ives " (Selden Society).

" on the religious side, the free fairs on the commer-
" cial side evoked and cherished the international
" spirit." [1] We ought to be able to say not less
(assuming the truth of this statement) about the
effect of the intercourse regulated by the courts of
the English seaports, but there are difficulties in
the way. For example, the preamble to the
statute, 9 Edward III., cap. 1 (1335) shows that the
seaports in particular did not share the King's
liking for the foreign merchant, a fact not to be
wondered at since, unlike the King, they did not
get much out of him. We read of " people of
" cities, boroughs, ports of the sea, and other places
" which in long time past have not suffered, nor
" yet will suffer Merchant Strangers," and so forth.
In 1349 we hear that two Spanish ships have been
seized in the port of Plymouth, not by ordinary
depredators, but " by the bailiffs of that town for
" trespasses done by Spaniards against the men
" of that town." [2] The merchants and masters of
the ships complain to the Council, and the King
appoints a sergeant-at-arms to release the vessels
from arrest, and to bring them to London : public
warning is to be given that all persons wishing to
complain against the said merchants and masters
are to be before the Council by the Feast of the
Ascension at the latest to prosecute their plaints.
The authorities of the town of Plymouth were
apparently extending the old idea of the " collective

---

[1] Art., " Fairs," *Enc. Brit.*
[2] Cal. Patent Rolls. April 24, 1349.

liability " [1] of gild or borough to the entire Spanish
nation, or at least the mercantile part of it. From
this account it seems probable that the courts of
the sea-boroughs, however useful locally, could not
always be trusted to " cherish the international
spirit." Where the matter is municipal, so to
speak, as regards the parties, the neighbours are
helpful. In 1385 three men of Bristol City quarrel
with a ship-master of Tenby : the commission
appointed to investigate the case includes the names
of several persons belonging to Bristol, and a writ
of aid for them is directed to the mayor and bailiffs
of the town.[2] But, as a Chancellor of near a
century later said in a case of a foreign suitor, the
law merchant is " *ley universal par tout le monde—le
ley de Nature.*" [3] As soon as it was discerned that
the law merchant and the law maritime, which, as
we have seen, were practically identical, had this
aspect of *ius gentium*, the little local courts of the
seaports, manned by bailiffs and " ministers " of
the town, may well have seemed inadequate for
their duties. How soon this happened one cannot
say ; but the reign of Edward the Third, when
the admirals' courts appear, was a period of increasing foreign commerce, of transition from
medieval to modern ideas, and a little blending of
Praetorian equity with Oleronian law may already
have been seen to have something to recommend

[1] See Pollock and Maitland, " Hist. of English Law," Vol. I.,
pp. 682, 683.
[2] Cal. Patent Rolls. Dec. 7, 1385, and Jan. 3, 1386.
[3] " Year Book," 13 Edw. IV., 9.

it. The lawyer learned in the Civil Law was best fitted to effect this.

Having suggested that possibly the old quay-side tribunals of the ports were already lagging behind the times, let us return to the courts of the admirals, newly set up. Where in the Patent Rolls an early deputy or judge has a description of his calling appended to his name it is not such as would lead us to suppose that he could improve upon the justice of the borough courts, either in the way indicated or any other. About 1347 a " king's yeoman," Philip de Witton, is " supplying the place of " the Admiral of the West.[1] He certifies that a ship belonging to Thomas Cok of Fawy is forfeited to the King for robbery committed upon the sea by the men therein, and the King gives it to Peter Foulk of Winchelsea " in compensation for " a ship of his which the King for certain causes " lately caused to be sunk in the port of Caleys." One would like to have been told more of the part that Foulk's ship had played in the operations against Calais, taken by the English in this year, but what more immediately concerns us is to note that the admiral's deputy is here exercising as much an administrative function as a judicial one, and if the office were at first so regarded it would account for the appointment of deputies without any particular legal training. But be that as it may, Andrew de Guldeford, the lieutenant of Ralph Spigurnell, warden of the Cinque Ports and admiral in 1366, is described as a " king's sergeant-

---

[1] Cal. Patent Rolls. Feb. 21, 1347.

at-arms." [1]   And in 1371 we have Walter Hanley,
" sergeant-at-arms," sitting as lieutenant of Robert
de Assheton, admiral of the King's fleet from the
Thames towards the west, on information that
evil-doers have attacked three ships of the merchants of Portyngale of the King's amity.[2]   He has
Richard de Lyouns, a London merchant, associated
with him, probably as assessor in a case concerning
merchant shipping, and following the ancient usage
in the constitution of the seaport courts. But
about 1390 the deputy of the admiral of the west
is a knight of the name of Nicholas Clifton who
plays his part alone. One Swanland appeals
against his decision in the matter of a bond made
" far inland and nowhere near the sea coast, in
" respect of which the appellant alleges that the
" said Nicholas has no jurisdiction, and moreover
" has pronounced sentence without citing him or
" giving him notice." [3]   After this one is not sur-
prised to find two other appeals from the knight's
sentences recorded in 1391.   This was the year in
which the second statute of Richard, forbidding
the encroachments of the admirals' deputies, was
passed ; and the irregularities committed by the
court of the Earl of Huntingdon, admiral in the
south and west, are supposed largely to have

---

[1] Cal. Patent Rolls. Jan. 30, 1366.   "Note that in later times
the Steward of the Lord Warden's court was regularly described
as ' *senescallus eruditus* ' ;   this court had Chancery as well as
Admiralty jurisdiction down to the eighteenth century, and the
steward, as the judge's delegate, had a position much like that
of a Master in Chancery."   Sir F. Pollock, Bart., K.C.

[2] Cal. Patent Rolls.   Dec. 3, 1371.

[3] Cal. Patent Rolls.   Dec. 12, 1390.

contributed to the need for it. During the previous
year this nobleman had run foul of the City of
London, and we have him complaining that the
mayor and sheriffs had done " divers duresses,
" grievances, disobediences or rebellions, and pre-
" judices to the office and court of admiralty and
" procured them to be done." [1] If such was the
tone adopted towards London, whose chief magis-
trate could ask Edward the Third to dinner, the
lesser ports may well have been alarmed. Between the admiralties themselves there is also
evidence of conflict ; it is complained in 1401 that
the lieutenant of the admiral of the west, Thomas
Rameston, has upset a judgment previously obtained before the deputies of the Earl of Worcester,
admiral of England.[2] Nor was it the admirals
alone who endeavoured to convey (in Pistol's
phrase) other people's jurisdictions: only nine years
after the passing of the statute, 27 Edward III.,
establishing the Mayor of the Staple, he has to be
reminded that the common law is not within his
province.[3] The suitors, actual or potential, must
have been sorely puzzled. In 1393 or thereabouts,
John Copyn, master of the *Gabriel* of St. Osyth,
sued two merchants for the freight on a cargo of
wine brought by him from Bordeaux to Gadenesse
in Essex. He alleged that he had sued them first
at common law and afterwards in the Admiralty
Court of the north without remedy before he tried

[1] Cal. Patent Rolls. Jan. 24, 1390.
[2] *Ibid.* June 14, 1401.
[3] 36 Edw. III., cap. 7.

the court of the Constable and Marshal, " who said they had no jurisdiction." [1] As the wine is not stated to have been in the nature of military stores, it is not clear why this determined mariner thought of the Constable and Marshal ; but it is refreshing to find that on this occasion at least they recognized their limitations. Later on, in 1409, this court is accused, in common with those of the admirals, of taking cognizance " *des choses triables par le Commune ley.*" [2]

There existed then at this time between the various jurisdictions having within their purview the foreign merchant and contracts made outside the realm a state of conflict and unintelligibleness much in need of regulation. The new courts of the admirals, with a sergeant-at-arms as judge, and a tendency to regard a plea to the jurisdiction as a " rebellion " were probably even less satisfactory than the tribunals presided over by the seaport bailiff, not always to be trusted to do right to a " despoiled " foreign plaintiff.[3] It is submitted that between the truculence of the one and the parochialism of the other (and some evidence has been given of both) the civil lawyers found within their own field an opportunity of which in a few years they took advantage. There is reason for thinking that the procedure of the gradually evolved principal court of Admiralty, which was certainly sitting in Southwark by 1410 [4] underwent

[1] Cal. Patent Rolls. Nov. 25, 1393.
[2] Rolls of Parliament, II Hen. IV.
[3] See the Stat. 2 Hen. V., cap. 6, establishing Conservators of the Truces.
[4] Rolls of Parliament, 2. Hen. IV., c. 61.

regulation about the year 1406 ; and it is significant
that about this time, namely, in 1408, we meet in
the Patent Rolls with the name of Master Henry
Bole, Doctor of Laws, whom Prynne sets down first
in his list of judges of the Court of Admiralty—
with an interval, it may be added, of seventy years
before he can find a second one.   It has, it is true,
been pointed out that except as a diplomatist, a
chancery clerk, or a teacher, the civilian could find
little to do in England, and that the Court of
Admiralty, even when it came into existence, could
not afford employment for many practitioners.[1]
But the local sessions of the admirals, existing even
after the principal court had been set up, would
and did make an opening for some of them as
deputies.   The subject-matter of the cases coming
before the admiral's courts was within the civilian
chancery-clerk's sphere : " spoil " and piracy cases,
to deal with which the Court of Admiralty was
originally instituted, as well as cases arising out of
the Law Merchant which the Court of Admiralty
soon took upon itself to decide, had long been
matters of appeal to the Chancellor.   There is,
moreover, direct evidence that in the year 1404
certain doctors of the civil law were called in to
assist at the hearing in the Chancery of a suit
which had been transferred thither by a writ of
supersedeas from the admiralty court of the West
on the petition of one of the parties.[2]   It is always

[1] Pollock and Maitland, " Hist. of English Law," Chap. V.
[2] Close Rolls, 5 Hen. IV., Part 1, m. 3.   The material part of
the record (which was kindly communicated to me by Mr.
W. H. B. Bird at the suggestion of Mr. R. G. Marsden) is as

the lawyer learned in a law that is not national whose advice is sought in such matters: the unknown author of that part of the " Black Book of the Admiralty," which is called *Ordo Iudiciorum* or *Praxis Curiae Admiralitatis*, is supposed to have been a civilian of the University of Bologna. It is material, moreover, to remember that as far back as 1339, Edward the Third had referred to three ecclesiastics (in whom a knowledge of the civil law might be presumed) for advice as to the laws proper to be enforced in maritime matters: they were Adam Murimuth, Official of the Court of Canterbury, Richard de Chadderly, Dean of the Arches, and Henry de Eddesworth, Canon of St. Paul's, and in this circumstance Sir Travers Twiss sees an omen of coming events.[1] There was, however, nothing very new in the mere allocation of sea-affairs to churchmen: Edward the First's employment of William de Grenefeld, Canon of York, in the matter of a marine treaty, has already been mentioned.[2] Even before his time they had employment in the sphere of naval administration, though hardly in this case in virtue of purely legal attainments. We read of William Wrotham, Archdeacon of Taunton, being Keeper of the King's Ships in the time of John, and of Friar Thomas of the Temple occupying a similar position under

follows:—" *videbatur iusticiariis et servientibus ad legem ac aliis peritis de concilio in Cancellaria existentibus, necnon quibusdam iuris civilis doctoribus qui ibidem de mandato (Regis) venerunt materiam in dicta peticione contentam in Cancellaria de iure discuti seu terminari non debere.*"

[1] " Black Book," Vol. II., p. xlii.
[2] *Supra*, p. 6.

Henry the Third.[1] But the reliance of Edward the
Third upon the judges of the ecclesiastical courts
in London for advice on the law of the sea is undoubtedly a landmark, having regard to the subsequent settlement of the civilians under the shadow
of St. Paul's Cathedral, the ultimate holding of the
Arches and the Admiralty Courts in the same Hall,
and the fact that as late as the year 1840 the Dean
of the Arches was by statute empowered to sit
for the Judge of the High Court of Admiralty.[2]

But to return to our period : there were signs of
a fresh stirring of the Roman Law in England
during the latter half of the fourteenth century.
The Study of the Civil Law had outgrown the disfavour with which the Church had at one time
regarded it.[3] It was in Edward the Third's reign
that the Chancellor began in his administration
of Equity to resort to the *Corpus Iuris* or to the
Roman elements in the Canon Law, for the elucida-
tion of principles.[4] In 1350 Trinity Hall had been
founded by the lawyer-bishop, William Bateman,
exclusively for the furtherance of the study of the
Civil and the Canon Laws : it was afterwards, as
we shall see, to have something to do not only
with the teaching of the civil law but with the
practising civilian lawyer. The fulminations of
John Wyclif against the Roman Law in the year

---

[1] " Black Book," Vol. II., p. xlii : as to Friar Thomas, see
Nicolas, " Hist. Royal Navy," Vol. I., p. 221.
[2] 3 & 4 Vict., cap. 65, s. 1.
[3] Clark, " Cambridge Legal Studies," p. 41.
[4] Goudy, " Fate of Roman Law North and South of the
Tweed," p. 15.

1378 may also be taken as proof of the existence of a revived interest in it. Without going so far as to say that at the epoch with which we are concerned the legal legacy of Rome (like certain art treasures from the Acropolis at a much later day) attained the doubtful dignity of an English party question, we know that Richard the Second's fondness for it caused the barons in Parliament to declare that this realm of England had never been and should never be ruled or governed by the civil law.[1] It seems a fair inference from these facts that an increase in the number and activity of the civilians was contemporary with them.

At all events, we have Master William Menesse, clerk, licentiate in laws, sitting as deputy or judge for the admiral in the West as early as 1391.[2] There are a few instances of knightly deputies afterwards, but, so far as added descriptions enable us to judge, one or even two clerics were usually their colleagues. And in 1403 there is Master Simon Sydenham, Doctor of Laws, sitting alone as Lieutenant and Commissary of the Admiral of the North;[3] in 1406 Master Thomas Felde, Doctor of Laws, described as " late commissary of " Henry, Lord of Beaumont, late sub-admiral in " the south and west," [4] and in 1408 there is Dr. Bole, already mentioned, Prynne's first judge, who is described in the Patent Rolls as Lieutenant of

---

[1] Blackstone's "Commentaries" :   (1765).   Introduction, p. 19.
[2] Cal. Patent Rolls.   June 20, 1391.
[3] *Ibid.*   Mar. 1, 1403.
[4] *Ibid.*   July 23, 1406.

Thomas Beaufort, knight, Admiral of England and
Ireland. It would not be difficult, if it were worth
while, partly to fill up from this source the long gap
in Prynne's list between Bole and one William Lacy,
LL.B., judge in 1483 ; but it is enough to say here
that from early in the fifteenth century the civilian
lawyer appears completely to have ousted the
" chivaler " and sergeant-at-arms from the Admiralty judgment seats, and to be nearly as frequently
appealed from. The statute of Henry the Fifth,
in 1414, whereby " two learned men in the law "
were always to be associated with the conservator
of the truces in the seaports, does not say which
law ; but it may have marked the exit of the un-
assisted and unlearned official. And the first
quarter of the century is but just gone when the
existence of a body of advocates practising in the
Admiralty Courts is indicated by the record of a
suit in 1430, before the admiral's deputy " in the
parts of Norfolk and Suffolk." [1] The defendant
" could not find a counsel there, and the admiral
" accordingly revoked the case to his principal court
" at Southwark near London, where counsel are in
" plenty, commanding his lieutenants or deputies in
" the said parts to proceed no further in the matter."

The principal court was still located at Horton's
Quay in Southwark in the time of Henry the Eighth,
afterwards moving to the church of St. Margaret-
at-hill in the same parish. Something of the way
in which the local courts like that in the parts of
Norfolk and Suffolk were co-ordinated with it may

[1] Cal. Patent Rolls. July 18 1430.

be surmised from the use of the word " revoked,'' which seems to imply that causes originally instituted in the principal court were sent down to the country deputies for trial. In the year 1410 the Commons had complained of people being summoned by the officers of the admiral " *à Loundres à le key de* William Horton, Suthwerke " ;[1] and in 1422 there is mention of a court of the admiral " held in turn at the towns of Dertemouth. Plymouth, and Kyngesbrygge." [2] If the deputies went small local circuits like this it throws fresh light upon the well-known anxiety of the boroughs to obtain grants of exemption from the jurisdiction of the admiral. But the most interesting fact that emerges from the record of the Norfolk case is that the Admiralty side of what afterwards became the College of Advocates was apparently ready for business by the year 1430. It may not have been a very numerous body. It is said that the doctors even when the college was established, only numbered sixteen or seventeen in 1585, and forty-four in 1694 :[3] but if the record just cited is to be believed there were already " plenty " under Henry the Sixth for the purpose of giving counsel.

How completely admiralty cases were regarded as the province of the civilians and canonists by the time the first quarter of the fifteenth century had passed may be gathered from the form of the commissions then issued to hear appeals from the

---

[1] Rolls of Parliament. 2 Hen. IV., s. 61.
[2] Cal. Patent Rolls. June 25, 1422.
[3] Thornbury, " Old and New London," Vol. I., p. 286.

D

admirals' deputies. There is one in 1429 to the famous canonist, William Lyndwode, therein described as a doctor of both laws, to Master John Lynfeld, bachelor in laws, and Master Senobius Noffre, doctor of decrees, together with two aldermen of London, to hear an appeal against a decision given by Doctor John Gentil, the lieutenant of the Admiral : but it goes on, " and to any two or more of them," always including either Lyndwode, or Lynfeld or Noffre, so that the lay members of the commission could never act by themselves.[1] Other commissions of about the same date contain the same precaution. The civil lawyer was now fully seised of his maritime demesne.

[1] Cal. Patent Rolls. Sept. 18, 1429.

III. THE FIFTEENTH CENTURY

The successors of the learned persons just mentioned had established themselves in London on something like a collegiate foundation—a small legal profession apart from the ordinary one— before the death of Henry the Seventh in 1509. The section of our story that is mainly concerned with the sixteenth century may be anticipated so far as to say that the records of what was in later times styled " The College of Doctors of Law exercent in the Ecclesiastical and Admiralty Courts " go back to the year 1511. But the way was being prepared for it long before. It is difficult not to associate the gradual emergence of this institution to full and formal establishment with currents of thought and culture that had begun to flow during the fifteenth century. Moreover, although admiralty and international law were but a part of the business of these practitioners it was within that province especially that those currents would seem to have helped the civilians on their course. There were political reasons also—when, later, we come to the time of Henry the Eighth, even reasons of ecclesiastical polity [1]—why the underlying principles of the civilians' science would meet with the temporary approval of statesmen. It will therefore not be out of place to refer to some

[1] See Maitland, " Canon Law in England "(1898), p. 92, *et seq*.

of the more characteristic tendencies of the age,
though such reference must needs be both brief
and superficial.

We learnt in our youth from the pages of Green's
" Short History " that when the lawyers of the
Long Parliament turned back to look for prece-
dents of constitutional liberty they found that the
hundred years or so between the accession of
Edward IV. and the time of Elizabeth yielded
nothing to their purpose. This is the period to
which the fifteenth century led up, and which it
partly overlaps. It was also a time of increasing
foreign commerce, of much advancement of learning,
and at its close coincided with a golden era of
literary accomplishment. It may perhaps be said
in palliation of that century's political short-
comings, which, however, appear not to have been
incompatible with progress in other directions, that
when a nation, or the more reputable and far-seeing
part of it, is faced by danger of anarchy it is apt to
welcome law and order howsoever provided. In
England in the middle of the fifteenth century the
old feudal basis of society was being shattered ;
and freedom had aforetime been won by the sword
of that very Baronage which was exhausting itself
in the Wars of the Roses. In the middle of the
fifteenth century the Church, in the presence of
Lollardry and Socialism, had ceased to be a great
political power ; and the Church in older days
had been the protector of the tradition of freedom.[1]
It would be fantastic to suppose that many con-

[1] Green, *op. cit.*, Chap. VI., Sect. iii.

temporary minds, even when confronted by cracks in the edifice of state so apparent, turned wistfully towards the coherence and permanence of the legal system of imperial Rome, with its un-English spirit. Yet if the above-mentioned changes paved the way, as we are told they did, for the absolutism of the Tudors, they would hardly dishearten the professed exponents of a code that contained the terse and convenient maxim, " *Quod principi placuit legis habet vigorem* " [1]—a phrase which Sir John Fortescue thrice quotes in his book in praise of the laws of England and always in order to show that no such principle of autocracy had any place in them. This text from Justinian's " Institutes " was a terrible and long lived *bête noire*.

The foreign trade of the country, moreover, was rapidly passing out of the hands of Hanseatic and Florentine merchants into those of Englishmen ; and the commercial classes demanded for their own ends above all things security and order. They desired, in particular, a uniform law, and they found it—or the civilians found it for them— in the *Corpus Iuris* : [2] " *Ius Iustiniani prae-scriptum libris, non civitatis tantum est, sed et gentium et naturae : et aptatum sic est ad naturam universum, ut imperio extincto, ipsum ius diu*

---

[1] " A maxim to which Glanvill had done lip-service before the Common Law found its own feet. Tudor statecraft bettered the instruction by reading " *princeps* " as the King in Parliament and working a practical despotism in strictly legal form. Fortescue, however, would probably have dissented from the doctrine of parliamentary omnipotence expounded by Sir Thomas Smith and now orthodox." Sir F. Pollock, Bart, K.C.

[2] Adams, " Civilisation during the Middle Ages," p. 449.

*sepultum surrexerit tamen, et in omnes se effuderit
gentes humanas*"—it was thus that Albericus
Gentilis wrote of it in the sixteenth century.[1] We
may perhaps add that at the beginning of the
fifteenth the obsequies of the Roman Empire were
so far incomplete that its ghost still occasionally
walked.   It is hard to say to what extent, if at all,
that august shade influenced practical men ; but
it is on record that when the Emperor Sigismund
landed at Dover in 1416 several nobles, including
Duke Humphrey of Gloucester, a great patron of
bookish folk, rode into the water to inquire whether
he claimed to exercise authority or jurisdiction in
England.   It is also said that a century later
Cuthbert Tunstall had to assure Henry VIII. that
he was no subject of the Empire, but an independent
sovereign.[2]   It may be that some of the doctors of
civil law of our period, behind the practical application of their science to international affairs, still
cherished the theory of a supreme central authority;
that sheet-anchor, so to speak, which, ever since
the Reformation created the independent modern
State [3] and upset Imperial and Papal applecart
alike, has been lacking to international lawyers.
" It was," says Bryce, " the Roman Empire and
" the Church taken together which first created
" the idea of a law common to all subjects and, later,

[1] De Jur. Bell., Lib. I., cap. 3.
[2] Dyer and Hassall, " Modern Europe," Vol. I., p. 23. " The
claim was, of course, much older in both England and France :
witness the title " Basileus " used here before the Norman
Conquest."   Sir F. Pollock, Bart, K C.
[3] " The supreme achievement of the Reformation is the modern
State."   Figgis, " Camb. Mod. Hist.," Vol. III., p. 736.

" to all Christians, a law embodying rights enforce-
" able in the courts of every civilised country." [1]
There may even have been a few men in England at
the beginning of the fifteenth century who were in
sympathy with Petrarch's words to the Roman
people in the middle of the fourteenth : " Was there
" ever such peace, such tranquillity, such justice
" . . . when was ever the State so wisely guided,
" as in the time when the world had obtained one
" head, and that head Rome ? " If so, they were
probably amongst the students of the Civil Law.
We allude in passing to this afterglow of Rome's
departed greatness only because it is still discernible
in the thought of the age. Doubtless both the
prestige and the usefulness of the *Corpus Iuris* were
already derived much more from those qualities
which Gentilis describes in the passage cited than
from a retrospect more or less sentimental.

We cannot say that the fact of there being no
longer any central political authority behind the
law " *et gentium et naturae* " which could be
gathered by the civilians out of their Roman books
accounts for English merchants at this period
bestirring themselves in an effort to bring about
some sort of law and order upon the sea. But the
measures taken in England at this time to that end
—chiefly directed to an increase of what is now
called sea-power—are not unrelated to our subject
inasmuch as such alternative remedy as might lie
in an appeal to law and reason rested, when and so
far as it was possible to apply it, in the hands of the

[1] "Studies in History and Jurisprudence," Vol. II., p. 130.

doctors of the civil law, either as diplomatists or as admiralty judges. It is evident, however, that the practical men of the fifteenth century had no great faith in law unbacked by force : nor does their want of enough force to put down the disorder at sea that characterised their time impeach the commonsense of their theory. If the law of nations and of nature did not work very well upon the high seas it was clearly expedient in any international difference, public or private, which might arise thereon to ensure as far as possible that your side should be the stronger. The alternative is probably inherent in the nature of things. It is possible that a more minute investigation into the origins of maritime jurisdiction would show that the imperfect sanction of *ius naturae* had a good deal to do with the well-known assertions of dominion over large tracts of salt water by particular sovereigns and states in medieval and even later times. Incidentally we might point to the antithesis of *ius naturale* and sea-power made as far back as the early years of the fourteenth century by a commentator on Bracton, whose gloss testifies, as Professor Maitland pointed out, to a very early claim on the part of the King of England to a lordship of the sea [1] " *Et nota de prima parte*," he wrote, " *quod in Anglia minus curatur de iure* " *naturali quam in aliqua regione de mundo quia* " *Rex Angliae vocatur dominus marium propter* " *potestatem suam quam habet in aquis.*" The note certainly testifies to the claim : but one may also

[1] Bracton and Azo.　(Selden Society, 1895), p. 125.

see in it something perhaps of the jurist's regret at
the supersession of " natural " law by national
power. To revert to the fifteenth century, however, there is no doubt about the opinion of the
author of " The Libel of English Policie, exhorting
" all England to keepe the sea and namely the
" narrowe sea," a rhymed tract which is ascribed to
a date between 1426 and 1437.[1] He is a thorough-
going nationalist ; he has nothing whatever to
say about the Law of Nature, but when once he
passes away from purely commercial topics, a good
deal about Edward the Third, his gold noble with
the ship on it, the naval victory off Sluys, and the
" great shippes " of Henry the Fifth. His doctrine
is that

> " The ende of battaile is peace sikerly
>   And power causeth peace finally,"

and he sees in an England strong upon the sea " an
endly or finall processe of peace by authoritie,"
which—and here the poet steps in—is to culminate
in every nation cultivating unity of spirit in the
bond of peace, conformably to the admonition of the
Apostle. It were easy to raise a smile at the good
man's optimism ; but at least he recognizes the
crucial necessity of a policeman, and the quaint
project of an International Navy had not been
thought of in his day. There have been much
later occasions when the strength of the British
Navy has come near to fulfilling the rôle he imagined
for it, and that not upon the " narrowe sea " alone.
But in truth the author of " De Politia Conserva-

[1] Printed in Hakluyt's " Principal Navigations."

tiva Maris " was thinking principally of England's particular interests, and already in 1415 the Commons in speaking of the Navy had placed on record their opinion that " *la dit Naveye est la griendre substance du bien, profit & prosperitee du vostre dit Roialme,*"[1] words which, as has been re-marked, anticipate by nearly 250 years those of the preamble to the Naval Discipline Act of 1661, and still have a close paraphrase in the Statute Book.

Measures showing a recognition of the importance of sea-power to commerce and of both to the Kingdom had already been taken. The growing merchant class in 1406, the same year in which the procedure of the Admiralty Court is supposed to have been regulated anew, were bent upon looking after the security of the trade-routes them-selves : and accordingly an enactment of that year placed the safeguard of the sea in the hands of the merchants, mariners and shipowners of England from the first of May to the Feast of St. Michael next-ensuing, and thence for the space of one year.[2] The ordinance contains some interesting provisions as to the ways and means of the scheme which must not now detain us : that it was temporary and experimental does not detract from its interest as a symptom. But the merchants, as Sir Michael Foster significantly puts it, were soon " eased of a " service they were found to be very unequal to, " their admirals' commissions dropped and the

[1] Rolls of Parliament, 3 Hen. V.
[2] Rolls of Parliament, 7 & 8 Hen. IV.

" whole direction of the marine returned to its
" proper channel." [1] Another extraordinary effort
to establish order at sea was made some fifty years
later in the reign of Henry the Sixth, and had no
more success than that of the merchants and shipowners in 1406. This time the Earls of Salisbury and
Oxford and other nobles took upon themselves the
keeping of the sea from April, 1454, for a term of
three years, " they to have for the said cause the
" subsidie of tonnage and poundage granted unto us
" at our last parlement " and, in addition, a sum of
2,000 marks " by way of rewarde." [2] Yet in spite
of all efforts to secure " peace by authoritie "
piracy continued to flourish : during the latter half
of the fifteenth century, English, French, Spanish,
Portuguese, Genoese, Venetian, Flemish and
German corsairs preyed upon the shipping of all
countries indiscriminately.[3] It will be apparent
from the facts adduced in the course of what may
have seemed a digression that the need of admiralty
courts to deal with piracy and " spoil " cases was
not less at the end of the fifteenth century than it
had been in the time of Edward the Third, who first
established them for that purpose 150 years before :
and the civil lawyers who had annexed those courts
had probably no lack of plaints with which to deal.

The reign of Henry the Fifth, at the beginning of
which the Commons had stated their pious opinion
of the King's Navy, was indeed marked by the

[1] " Reports," 2nd Ed., p. 168.
[2] Stevenson, " Papers *temp*. Henry VI.," Vol. II, ," pp. 493-4.
[3] Marsden, " Select Pleas in the Court of Admiralty," p. lvi.

promulgation of regulations in virtue of which Stubbs does not hesitate to call that sovereign " the " founder of our military, international and maritime " laws "[1] : and we may be pretty sure that in the framing of them the professors of the Civil Law would be consulted, following the precedent, already alluded to, set by Edward the Third. The Statute of Truces in the second year of Henry's reign was passed with the object of regulating maritime warfare by forbidding all acts of violence on the main sea without the authority of the King, and by requiring captors of ships to bring their prizes into port for adjudication.[2] It was found to have gone a little too far, and to have made the King's subjects afraid of attacking the King's real enemies ; it was followed in the fourth year of the reign by a statute authorizing the issue of letters of marque and reprisal under the Great Seal.[3] Besides these efforts to regulate the proceedings of his lieges at sea Henry built a Navy, and possessed in the year 1417 six great ships, eight barges and ten balingers.[4] There is also to his credit the Ordinances of War drawn up in 1419, a more elaborate and, for the times, a more enlightened code of military law than had previously appeared.[5] We may here again assume with some certainty the assistance of the civil lawyers. The laws of

[1] " Constitutional History," Vol. III., p. 77.
[2] 2 Hen. V., cap. 6.
[3] 4 Hen. V. cap. 7.
[4] Nicolas, " Agincourt," App., p. 21. The " barges " were rigged with one mast like the ships and carried guns.
[5] Printed in their earliest English form in Twiss, " Black Book of the Admiralty," Vol. I., App., p. 459.

war had always been one of their special subjects,
and the Court of the Constable and Marshal which
administered them regulated its proceedings by
the civil law. Concerning this now obsolete court
little need be added to the account of it that
Blackstone gives. The Court of Chivalry was a
military court or court of honour when held before
the Earl Marshal only ; it was also a criminal
court when held before the Lord High Constable of
England jointly with the Earl Marshal, and then
it had jurisdiction over pleas of life and member
arising in matters of arms and deeds of war as well
out of the realm as within it.[1] But the passage in
which Serjeant Hawkins notices it may be cited,
since it throws considerable light on the limited use
of the civil law in England. The Court of the Constable and Marshal, he says, " ought to follow its
" own Customs and Usages so far as they go, and
" in cases omitted the Rule of the Civil Law." We
have here an exact analogy to the supplementing
of the Sea customs in the admiralty courts : the
" customs and usages " of the Court of Chivalry
were at the same time gradually embodied in such
Ordinances as that just mentioned which Henry
the Fifth promulgated, or were set forth in books
like the " De Studio Militari " of Nicholas Upton,
Bachelor both of Civil and Canon Law, who wrote
in the first half of the fifteenth century, and " The
Practice, proceedings and lawes of armes " which
Matthew Sutcliffe, Dean of Exeter and an advocate
at Doctors' Commons, brought out at the end of

[1] " Commentaries." (1765) Book IV. Chap. XIX. p. 264.

the sixteenth.   Hawkins proceeds : " And yet the
" Judges of the Common Law take notice of the
" jurisdicton of this Court, and give credit to a
" certificate of its Judges for the trial of an issue
" concerning its Proceedings : for the Civil Law
" is as much the Law of the Land, in such Cases
" wherein it has been always used, as the Common
" Law is in others." [1]   As showing further that
the law military was one of the civilians' special
provinces a reference may be made to John Ferne's
description of a trial by combat before the Court
of the Constable and Marshal, in his " Blazon of
Gentrie," published in 1586.   At the feet of the
judges on such an occasion he tells us " shal be
" placed a competent number of auncient and
" experienced Knights, with the King of Heraldes,
" and one Doctor or more of the Civill Lawes, to
" assist the Court in advise concerning the lawes
" of battaile and combat if anye thing of difficultie
" should then happen." [2]   An antiquated regulation, even when Ferne wrote : but still, when in
1631 the Court of the Constable and Marshal was
revived *ad hoc* for the trial of an appeal of treason
committed out of the realm (by the temporary
appointment of the Earl of Lindsay as Lord High
Constable) the civilians duly made their appearance: Dr. Dethick was registrar, Dr. Duck appeared
as the King's Advocate, and Dr. Eden was of
counsel for the appellee.[3]   As to the court of
chivalry held before the Earl Marshal only, it was

---

[1] 2 Hawk., P. C., cap. 4, sect. ii.
[2] *Op. cit.*, p. 324.   [3] Rea *v.* Ramsay, 3. St. Tr., p. 483

voted a grievance by the House of Commons in
1640 ; and the criminal court of the Constable and
Marshal had long been obsolescent because it could
not be constituted without the Constable—an
office never regularly filled up after Henry the
Eighth's time. Nevertheless we shall find the
doctors of the civil law still giving active assistance
in administering the laws, not of private but of
public war, in the reign of Charles the Second.[1]

In endeavouring to estimate the reinforcement
that the position of the English civilians probably
received before the middle of the fifteenth century
had passed one should not leave out of account
their intercourse with Italy, the original home of
the study they professed. There was Thomas
Beckington, for instance, afterwards Bishop of
Wells. He was the judge of the Arches Court in
1423, and sat upon several commissions to hear and
determine Admiralty appeals between 1428 and
1443.[2] It is of interest to note that in the year
1433, an appeal in a collision case wherein a ship
called *le Antony* of London had been injured came
before Beckington and other commissioners.[3]
Beckington is described in one of these appointments in 1439 as doctor of laws and decrees. His
correspondence with learned men in Rome is still
extant, and Rome from the time of Nicholas V. to
that of Leo X.[4] had again become the world's
centre. There were other Englishmen who were

[1] *Infra*, p. 102.
[2] Cal. Patent Rolls, *passim*.
[3] Cal. Patent Rolls. Oct. 20, 1433.
[4] 1447–1513. Beckington died in 1465.

not only in touch with the scholars of the Renaissance through the post, but had resided for years in Italian centres of learning before holding high office at home. Such an one was William Grey, afterwards Bishop of Ely, appointed by Henry VI his proctor at the Roman Curia. Twenty years later, in 1449, he became Lord High Treasurer. John Tiptoft, Earl of Worcester, must also be mentioned because he learnt more in Italy than Englishmen approved of, and learnt it in the domain of law. Tiptoft had attended lectures at Venice, Padua, Florence, and Rome before he came to preside in the Court of the Lord High Constable from 1462 to 1467. When in 1470 he met with the fate to which he had condemned many others and was beheaded on Tower Hill, we are told by his biographer, the Florentine bookseller, Bisticci, that the mob cried out that he deserved to die because he had brought into England the law of Padua—*law padowe*, as Warkworth has it. The civil law, as we have seen, might properly be drawn upon in the Court of the High Constable, but the Earl, no doubt, combined great cruelty with his foreign learning. He was an early example of the Italianate Englishman, who was described a little later, when the type became more common, as a devil incarnate. But the story illustrates the contemporary English bias against imported methods of judicature, even if the mob attributed to culture what was really due to heartlessness. There is a wide difference, of course, between Tiptoft's judicial butcheries and the application of foreign law maxims

by the civilians to matters already admitted to
appertain to their sphere ; and yet some adroitness
on the part of the doctors of the civil law in England
may have been necessary in order to avoid awaken-
ing what Pardessus, *à propos* of the admiralty
courts, has called " *l'espèce de repugnance que les
Anglais ont, en général, pour l'usage du droit
romain.*" [1]

It is remarkable that the Roman law does not
seem to have been as much as mentioned at Westminster. The allusions by Parliament to the courts
exercising a maritime jurisdiction in the early part
of the fifteenth century give no hint of any foreign
tincture in their procedure. " *Solonc ce qe la Ley
& Custume du Meer demaundent.*" " After the
old custom and law on the main sea used " are
the phrases we read.[2] And when the Commons in
1413 petitioned that the decision of a case involving
points of international law which had occurred at
sea might be committed by the King to his Court
of Admiralty, it was " *pur estre la determine, dis-
" cusse & ajugge solonq la ley, bons & droiturelx
" usagez & custumez de dit Court.*" [3] Cruelty by a
master to a mariner is alleged in 1445 to be " *contra
leges maritimas et statutum de Oleron.*" We are a long
way yet from the admission made in Edward VI.'s
reign (diplomatically and to a foreigner, it should
be owned) that English maritime legal practice
was nothing but the civil law together with certain
customs of the realm. Still, as a matter of legal

[1] Lois Maritimes. Vol. IV., p. 197.
[2] Rolls of Parliament, 7 & 8 Hen. IV. ; 2 Hen. V., cap. 6.
[3] Rolls of Parliament, 1 Hen. V.

E

history, it has perhaps hardly been enough em-
phasised that in admiralty and international
matters, through the various influences to which
allusion has been made, the tide was during the
fifteenth century strongly setting in from the
southward.

One feature of the case that the Commons, as
above mentioned, asked to have referred to the
Court of Admiralty may be pointed out as seeming
to afford evidence of this tendency. The facts
have been recorded in some detail, and are interesting not only as providing a strangely modern
picture of nautical procedure in the exercise of the
right of visit and search, but also because they show
that the prize law under which an English com-
mander acted at this date was that of the Mediterranean Consolat del Mar. The "*statutum de
Oleron*," the old maritime common law of North-
Western Europe, the code, as we have seen, of the
English maritime courts, does not concern itself
with such high matters as prize of war : but it is
none the less significant to find principles which
are laid down in the more elaborate code of the
south adopted when the occasion arose by an
English officer, because it looks as if they must
already have received the approval of the authorities at home. Sir H. Nicolas describes a similar
instance of the exercise of the right of searching
neutral vessels, which occurred in 1442, and which
he culls from Beckington's Journal of his Mission
to the Count of Armagnac, as an "important historical fact." The historical importance in both

cases consists in the adoption in practice by the English of Mediterranean law. The " Consolat del Mar " was printed at Barcelona before the end of the century ; a fact which implies a considerable antecedent demand for copies.

Eight ships belonging to English merchants, being at Bordeaux in the way of trade, were requisitioned by order of the Duke of Clarence for the purpose of bringing back to England from that port a number of soldiers and other persons. For the good and substantial guard and governance of the said people, ships, and effects, as the record puts it, one John Colvyle, Knight, was made Captain and Governor for the voyage. As the eight ships were proceeding peaceably on their way they met near Belle Isle with two " Hulks of Pruse," bound for La Rochelle, laden with wines and other merchandise. In order to ascertain whether these vessels and their cargoes were going to the King's enemies Colvyle dispatched to them a boat with one of his esquires and two master-mariners of his fleet, commanding the masters and merchants on board the strangers to produce their charters of affreightment, and informing them, moreover, that any goods of the enemy must be delivered up to Colvyle, he agreeing to pay the freight in respect of them (" *lour ferreit gree & paiement pur la freit d'icell* "). The hulks' people would not answer ; but the next day, according to the story told, they suddenly became warlike and made an attack on Colvyle's ships and killed some of his company. Thereupon Colvyle captured the hulks, and brought them with their cargoes into Poole and Southampton. The questions the decision of which was sought were whether or not on the facts stated the two hulks of Pruse ought to be forfeited as well as the goods in them, and secondly, whether or not the owners of the eight requisitioned merchant ships were entitled to both as good and lawful prize (" *sount dignez d'avoir icelles Hulks & Merchandisez* "). As to the first point, if the cargoes of the Prussian vessels were in fact enemy property they were clearly within Chapter CCXXXI of the " Consolat del Mar " ; as to the second, one may remember that even down to Armada times requisitioned merchantmen formed the bulk of the national fighting navy.

It is doubtful whether the other prize-law principle of the Consolat that neutral goods should go free in enemy ships (subject as therein mentioned) was ever the accepted English policy,[1] but the fact of a statute being passed in 1442 expressly repudiating it [2] may be evidence that there was a likelihood about that time of its adoption by English admiralty courts.

Appeals from the Admiralty Courts were to the King in Chancery, and were heard by special commissioners, " *iudices delegati*," appointed upon each occasion, who were invariably civilians.[3] This practice was copied into the statute of Henry the Eighth which put a stop to appeals to Rome from

[1] Westlake, " International Law," Part II., p 124.
[2] 20 Hen. VI., cap. 1.
[3] Marsden, " Select Pleas," Vol. I., p. lxxix.

the ecclesiastical courts [1] and accounts for the name of the Court of Delegates, the appellate tribunal for ecclesiastical matters, until its jurisdiction was transferred to the Privy Council in 1832. In the fifteenth century appeals in admiralty cases to the commissioners delegated to try them seem to have protracted the litigation for a long time. That in the collision case of *le Antony* of London is first mentioned in 1433, though how long before that the suit had commenced we are unable to say; in 1437, however, exactly four years afterwards, another commission is appointed to determine it. [2] And there began some time prior to the year 1441, before Richard Mannyng, the Lieutenant of the Admiral, a suit between John Wauton, a fishmonger of London, and one Robert Chapman, vaguely described as of the county of York, about a cargo of salt. Both parties appealed from Mannyng's sentence, and the matter was only terminated in 1444 by the outlawry of Wauton at the suit of somebody else upon a plea of debt. The original judgment for £220, which he had obtained against Chapman, and which he deemed insufficient, had not yet been executed, owing, it may be, partly to Chapman's dexterity in getting two successive commissions appointed to hear his side of the question. Wauton's judgment-debt being forfeit to the Crown on his outlawry, we are informed that the King hearing " that the recovery of the sum " proceeded against conscience, pardoned Robert

[1] See 25 Hen. VIII., cap. 19, sect. iv.
[2] Cal. Patent Rolls. Oct. 16, 1437.

" the said sum and granted to him the same." [1]
With these records before us the custom of the
admiralty courts of first instance to sit by the
water-side in order to facilitate the dispatch of
maritime business has a certain irony. But then
it had other uses. There is mention of an excuse
put forward in those days by a not very con-
vincing person who had been cited before a local
admiralty court and had failed to appear there.
He pleaded that instead of its being "kept" upon
the quay it had, against all precedent, retired into
the interior of the town, and that therefore he was
unable to find it.

A closer interest of the Crown in the Admiralty
Court towards the end of the century is shown by
the grant during pleasure in 1482 to the King's
servant Robert Rydon of " the office of King's
" promoter of all causes, criminal and civil or
" concerning crimes of *lese majestie*, before the
" King's judges of the constableship and Ad-
" miralty of England with all accustomed profits
" and 20 marks yearly from the receipt of the
" Exchequer." In the year following the same
office is granted for life to Master William Buller,
notary, at the like salary.[2] In the next year, 1484,
Rydon is appointed along with William Lacy,
bachelor in laws, already chief judge in the admiralty court, and others, a commissary-general in
the office of the Admiralty of England, with power
to try cases both civil and criminal : and the

[1] Cal. Patent Rolls. Oct. 30, 1441 ; Jan. 26, 1442 ; Feb. 4
1444.
[2] *Ibid.* Oct. 23, 1482 ; Dec. 10, 1483.

Commissaries are to engage a notary " to write out all that they do." [1] It is unfortunate that the writings of this notary are lost, because no record of any other appointment similar to that of these Commissaries is forthcoming. It indicates, as Mr. Marsden has pointed out, that the High Court of Admiralty was not even yet an efficient tribunal, since the " commissaries-general " must have been intended to exercise some of the functions of its Judge.[2] And in fact Rydon is styled " *Iudex Admiralitatis* " in a record of a case before the Court of Requests in the year 1495.

The Court of Requests, which had started by being a Committee of the Council—" the poor man's court of equity " is a description of its original function—was also captured by the civilians, probably before the end of the fifteenth century.[3] At any rate, amongst the lawyers who sat as Masters of Requests during the sixteenth will be found the names of all the most prominent civilians of the time. They include those of Christopher Middleton, John Tregonwell, William Cooke, David Lewis and Valentine Dale, each of them at some time also Judge in the Court of Admiralty, like their successor in both capacities Sir Julius Caesar, who published in 1597 a book upon " The Ancient State, Authoritie and Proceedings of the Court of Requests." Its procedure, he informs us, was

[1] Cal. Patent Rolls. April 8, 1484.
[2] " The Vice-Admirals of the Coast," *Eng. Hist. Rev.*, XXII., p. 471.
[3] Carter, " History of English Legal Institutions," 4th Ed., p. 170.

"altogether according to the process of summary causes in the civil law." It also had an admiralty jurisdiction well established in Henry the Seventh's time which was delegated to it from the Council. Caesar gives in the work alluded to a few records of " admirall causes " in the Court of Requests, as well as of certain cases he quaintly terms " ultra-marine," because they came from Calais or the Channel Islands. The facts related in one or two of the admiralty cases, which nearly all belong to the last years of the fifteenth century and so come within the scope of this section, may be here trans-scribed as showing the character of the civilians' practice in admiralty at this period. We have no records of the Admiralty Court proper until some thirty years later : and these, at any rate, show the extent to which depredations at sea and the remedy by way of reprisal still occupied the attention of judges who dealt with maritime affairs. In March, 1495, there is a mandate to the bailiffs of Wey-mouth to do right to Jaques le Maiore in the matter of the restitution of his ship. In April of the same year a Dane who had been detained on suspicion of piracy is released after swearing on the holy Evangelists that he will not afterwards molest any of the King's subjects *pro causâ suae incarcerationis*. On the same day John Whale of Winchelsea is granted a licence to take " *in aliqua parte maris, navem seu naves de Denmarke* ", and to bring them into port and retain them until satisfaction is made to him for the value of certain merchandise of his, *per inhabitantes de Denmarke minus juste captarum et detentarum.* Whale seems to have been a man of action : for only four days later comes the record of a decree assuring to him the possession of a ship he has arrested, " *quae navis venit ex partibus Denmarkiae,*" but subject to his giving bail to the Judge of the Admiralty Court to account for the ship or its value, such value to be determined by the appraisement of four indifferent persons. It may be, of course, as the date of Whale's exploit is not stated, that his licence to stop Danish ships was designed to give him an *ex post facto* justification of it : we cannot tell. In March of 1496 a Spanish merchant, one Martin Gavelino, brings a charge of plundering a ship called *La Mary,* " *in periculo infra le Goodwine sandes in mari,*" against a large number of defendants hailing from Dover, Kingsdown, Sandwich, Deal, Walmer, and Saint Margaret's ; these gentry, however, succeed in persuading the court that they were really salving Martin's merchandise and claim to be rewarded for their pains. The evidence upon which the Court decided that the animus of the defendants was innocent and even praiseworthy is not given ; we can only remark that in such cases it is still occasionally ambiguous. An award for salvage is made ; but Gavelino is to be given an opportunity of bringing further proof of spoliation if he can get it. As the whole district seems to have been involved, we imagine this to have been unlikely. These cases supplement what may be gathered from certain of the " Paston Letters," ascribed to the year 1491, as to the state of things at sea in the last decade of the fifteenth century. The Lord High Admiral seems to have been then kept fairly busy with reports of disorder and disputes involving questions of international law. We learn that the King of Denmark has complained to Henry VII. of robbery and extortion by English fishermen in Iceland : certain " men of warre," believed to be Danes, are upon the coast of England committing robberies, probably by way of reprisal : " certayne Corvers of Holand and Selond " are alleged to have been molested by an English shipmaster, and the Admiral is holding the owner of the English ship to bail.[1]

There would seem then to have been no lack of employment at this time for civilians who were inclined to specialize in maritime and international questions. Perhaps it may appear also from what we have noted of the fifteenth century that some of the difficulties that underlie the maintenance of a reign of international law—difficulties to which an age of supposed progress lately awoke with a shock—are really of quite respectable antiquity. *Eadem sunt omnia semper.*

[1] Gairdner, Ed. Vol. VI. Letters, 1046, 1047, 1049–51.

IV. THE RISE OF THE COLLEGE OF
ADVOCATES

We have already seen how it came about that the civilians had been able to establish themselves in the Admirals' courts ; it was considered that in the storehouse of the Roman Law principles might be found for the settlement of disputes to which the common law with its merely territorial incidence was technically inapplicable. It has also been noticed that since the civil and the canon laws were more or less co-extensive with Christendom, the learned in them had always been diplomatists, sent to argue with the foreigner. Civilian judge and state-envoy are, at the beginning of the sixteenth century, almost the same thing. John Clerk, a doctor of law of Bologna, and judge in the Court of Star Chamber, is ambassador to Rome in 1521, Master of the Rolls in 1522, and again ambassador to France in 1526. The Robert Rydon, already mentioned, who was made a commissary-general in the office of the Admiralty of England in 1484, is appointed in 1499, when he is described as Clerk of the Council and " Vice-Admiral of England," to be a plenipotentiary for the conclusion of peace with James of Scotland.[1]

[1] Cal. Patent Rolls. May 10, 1499.

The civilian not only concludes treaties, but assists judicially to carry them out. Christopher Middleton, Bachelor of Laws, who some seven years earlier had become the judge or deputy of the Admiral, was appointed in 1519, along with Cuthbert Tunstall, Master of the Rolls—himself a graduate in laws of Padua, the fountain-head of Roman Law at this time—to hear and determine all civil causes between the King's subjects and those of Francis I., in accordance with the treaty between the two sovereigns of the 4th October, 1518.[1] The end of Henry the Seventh's reign had coincided roughly with the change in international usage when the despatch of diplomatic envoys for special occasions began to be superseded by the permanent residence of ambassadors at foreign courts. The professors of the civil law were equally marked out for service under the new conditions. One need only instance the activities of the worldly-wise Dr. Nicholas Wotton, " *iuris ecclesiastici et civilis professor*," as he was officially described in 1536, who contrived to be employed both as envoy and ambassador during the four reigns of Henry, Edward, Mary, and Elizabeth, despite the various policies at home of those successive sovereigns. It may be recalled that his nephew, Sir Henry Wotton, is the reputed author of the jest, " *Legatus est vir bonus, peregre missus ad mentiendum Reipublicae causâ*," and perhaps a good man placed in such times might reasonably consider his own interest to be on

---

[1] " Letters and Papers " Hen. VIII., Vol. III., p. 89 ; Rymer, "Foedera." Vol. XIII. 700.

occasion identical with the commonwealth's. There are, indeed, other examples of the adroitness of the doctors in trimming their sails to the veering winds of doctrine. Tunstall himself was somewhat of a time-server, or, to put it another way, he displayed an "invincible moderation." We hear that Dr. Tregonwell is plucked from the Admiralty Court and the Arches by Henry the Eighth as the very man to be employed about the business of the Divorce and in the matter of the Dissolution of the Monasteries; yet he seems to have been still favoured after Mary had come to the throne. Almost the last employment in Mary's reign of Dr. Harvey, of whom we shall hear more, was his endeavour to rehabilitate Cardinal Pole in the Pope's favour; nevertheless he is Dean of the Arches under Elizabeth, and ten years after her accession, albeit suspected of an affection for the old religion, is prominent enough to take a leading part in establishing the advocates in their college in Knightrider Street. It may be charitably supposed that the doctors were of the same detached mind with their French contemporary and colleague, Cujas, who, when taken to task for his indifference to current controversies, is said to have replied, "*Nihil hoc ad edictum praetoris.*" But, at any rate, we may surmise that the practising civilian of Tudor times had perforce to be more than merely book-learned. That, no doubt, he was : nor must we omit, in order to complete our outline of his province, to mention his purely legal work in chambers. Five civilians were consulted in the case of the Bishop of Ross, envoy of Mary Stuart; and Dr. Valentine Dale's historical report to Burghley, " Notes on wars in ancient and modern times which have been commenced unlawfully or without sufficient cause " may be here alluded to, even if it has not entirely settled the questions with which it deals.

It was due to the long previous monopoly by the civilians of such employments as we have mentioned that their College, when started early in the sixteenth century, became what it was during the two centuries following. We may from this point with more aptness confine ourselves to the doctors of civil law, though many of them were still, like Wotton, doctors *utriusque iuris*, because the scope and prestige of the canon law were henceforward much restricted by the action of Henry the Eighth. If the doctors had been merely canonists and had subsided after the Reformation into a body of practitioners in the ecclesiastical courts of the English state church, it is hardly conceivable that Doctors' Commons would have produced jurists like Duck and Zouche, the " second Founder of the Law of Nations," or judges like Jenkins and Stowell, or that, as happened more than once during the eighteenth century, certain of its members would have been invited to assist the Court of King's Bench by argument before it.[1] Incidentally it may be stated that Dr. Thomas Oughton

---

[1] See Le Caux *v.* Eden. 2 Doug., p. 594, note : Rous *v.* Hassard, cited 2 Doug., p. 602, and Anthon *v.* Fisher, 3 Doug., p. 166. The practice was again made use of in 1845. *Vide infra*, p. 107.

in his " Ordo Iudiciorum " written in 1728, says
that on such occasions the doctors as a mark of
distinction were always admitted within the bar—
" *intra Cancellos in Foro (honoris gratia) semper
admittuntur.*"

The housing of this association of civil lawyers
in London was, as already stated, roughly contemporary with the highwater mark of the threatened
incursion of Roman Law into England in good
earnest ; and some attempt must be made to show
how far that movement went before we pass on
to merely topographical details. The last are of
interest chiefly as showing how closely the neighbourhood in which the College took root was
associated with the Latin-using, cosmopolitan
republic of letters to which the revival of learning
had given birth, and also (perhaps as a corollary)
with the international courtesies of the time. The
house in Knightrider Street in which the civilians
ultimately settled was that of William Blount,
fourth Lord Mountjoy, the patron and benefactor
of Erasmus on his first visit to England. Thomas
Linacre had first gathered the College of Physicians
together in his house in the same street in the year
1518. As to the reception of foreign notables, it
is said that when the Emperor Charles V. came to
London in 1522 his suite were lodged in, amongst
other places, Doctors' Commons itself. It was to
the houses round about St. Paul's Church, too, that
in 1559 the French Ambassadors, de Montmorency
and de Vielleville, were escorted by the nobility of
the English Court, and " found their lodgings

excellently provided with convenient rooms and
provisions for making good cheer." [1]

Diplomacy and the administration of justice in
matters arising on or beyond the four seas had
already been for ages the occupation of the civilian :
but his influence within the realm was again waxing
great.   We have remarked that the need for strong
government that followed upon the anarchy of the
Wars of the Roses tended to reinforce the prestige
of the Roman wisdom in the view of those who
counselled the Crown.   The democratic common
law inevitably received a check ; in the words of
Professor Nys " *la domination du droit national
parut menacée.*"

The threatened " reception " of the Roman Law
in England in the early part of the sixteenth century
and the reasons why in this country, unlike France,
Scotland and Germany, the movement never got
beyond a threat, were sketched with equal charm
and learning by the late Professor Maitland in his
Rede Lecture on " English Law and the Renaissance."   He says it is not a simple story ; and
certainly if one tries to discover the orientation, so
to speak, of the two camps favouring respectively
the English common law and the Roman civil law
with the great parties of the time, one is met at
once by puzzling cross-currents.   Upon the whole,
it seems that to have been in favour of the introduction of the civil law was, as Maitland in another
place puts it, a mark " of enlightenment and sometimes of advanced Protestantism, for your common

[1] Cal. S.P.   Venetian, Vol. VII., p. 16.

lawyer was apt to be medievally and even popishly
inclined." [1] It was one of the demands of the
Catholic insurgents during the Pilgrimage of Grace
" that the common law may have place as was used
at the beginning of the reign " ; on the other hand,
it was Reginald Cardinal Pole, who never ceased
trying to heal the breach between Henry and the
Vatican, who recommended that the civil law of
the Romans should become the common law of
England.[2] So that it would be probably true to
say that the civil law appealed to the enlightened
rather than to the populace.   It is also to be borne
in mind that Henry had been exalting the civil law
at the Universities.   It is even said that he lent
the light of his presence to the law lectures of Vives
at Oxford in 1523 and took Catherine with him.[3]
Professor Maitland has pointed out that the theory
of Church and State which the civilian found in
his books exactly suited Henry's ecclesiastical
policy.   He certainly suppressed at the same time
the study of the ancient canon law.   " King
" Henry," says Fuller, " stung with the dilatory
" pleas of the canonists at Rome in point of his
" marriage, did in revenge destroy their whole hive
" throughout his Universities."   But there was
more in it than pique : the suppression of the
canonist connoted the rise of the civilian.   " The

[1] " Collected Papers," Vol. III., p. 78.

[2] Starkey's " Dialogue between Pole and Lupset," Early
English Text Society.

[3] Jortin's " Life of Erasmus," Vol. I., p. 207. Vives was
incorporated D.C.L. in 1523, but the subject of his lectures and
the fact of Henry's attendance are alike doubtful.

F

" most superbly Erastian of all Henry's grandiose
" preambles," says Maitland, " introduces a
" statute that benefits the doctors of the civil law.
" They would not be ungrateful." [1]   What would
appear to have been the effect of Henry's
manoeuvres is curious.   There was a close connexion, exemplified in " Doctors' Commons " itself,
between the ecclesiastical courts administering
canon law and the admiral's court proceeding
according to civil law.   It is noteworthy that
Henry's action in Church matters was contemporary with an assertion by the Admiral of a jurisdiction in maritime and commercial affairs more
extensive than he had ever ventured upon before.
The legislation of Richard the Second, safeguarding
the rights of the common law, is scouted by the
patent granted to Henry Duke of Richmond,
Lord High Admiral in 1525, which confers a wide
jurisdiction, " *aliquibus statutis, actubus, ordina-
tionibus sive restrictionibus in contrarium non
obstantibus.*" [2]   Again, Henry's suppression of the
smaller monasteries led to insurrections in the
North of England, in consequence of which the
Council of the North was set up at York in 1537
with a criminal jurisdiction in Yorkshire and four
other counties as to riots, conspiracies and acts of
violence ;   and there seems always to have been a
sprinkling of doctors of the civil law amongst its
members from that time until its abolition in 1641.[3]

[1] " Canon Law in England," p. 92.   See 37 Hen. 8, c. 17.
[2] Marsden, " Select Pleas in the Court of Admiralty," Vol. I.,
pp. lvii., lviii.
[3] See Drake, " Eboracum " (1736), p. 368.

The Council was always obnoxious to the common lawyers; and the local justices, on one or two occasions at least, resented its interference.[1] Cuthbert Tunstall was its President in 1538.

The position which the civilians had attained by the time of the first Tudors was watched with no little jealousy by the ordinary lawyer. It was the complaint in 1546 of " divers studentes of the Commen Lawes of this realme " against a further invasion of the Court of Chancery by the civilians which gave to the Protector Somerset his opportunity to get rid of his rival the Earl of Southampton, Lord High Chancellor. In times past the influence of the civilian and canonist had not been unknown in that Court, nor was Somerset wanting in appreciation of the usefulness (as the world then went) of the Roman Law to the State, as he abundantly showed only two or three years later. But the Chancellor had made a slip in issuing a commission without warrant from the Council to certain persons to hear cases in Chancery, and after the judges had been consulted as to his fault he was deprived of the Seal. The fact that three of the four persons named in the commission were civilians was not the offence before the Council, though it dominates the complaint of the common lawyers, whose language is sufficiently instructive to warrant a transcription of a part of it.

" Pleasith it your honorable Lordships," they begin, " to call to your remembrance that whereas

[1] See " The Yorkshire Archaeological and Topographical Association." Record Series. Vol. III.

" the Imperial Crowne of this realme of Inglande
" and the hole estate of the same have been alwayes
" from the beginning a Reame (*sic*) Imperial having
" a lawe of itself called the Commen Lawes . . . "
This adroit use of the word "imperial" is noteworthy ; Henry the Eighth had affected the style
to show his independence of alien jurisdictions,
and it marks what the students were afraid of.
They go on to complain "that now of late this
" Commen Lawes of this realme, partely by In-
" junctions, aswel before verdictes, jugementes and
" execucions as after, and partly by Writtes of
" Sub Pena issuing owte of the Kinge's Courte
" of Chauncery, hath not been only stayed of their
" directe course but also many tymes altrid and
" violated by reason of Decrees made in the saide
" Court of Chauncery, moste grounded upon the
" Lawe Civile, and upon matter depending in the
" conscience and discretion of the hearers thereof,
" who, being Civilians and not lerned in the
" Commen Lawes, setting aside the saide Commen
" Lawes, determyne the waighty causes of this
" realme according either to the said Lawe Civile
" or to their owne conscience ; which Lawe Civile
" is to the subjects of this realme unknown. . . . "
Then follows the immediate grievance ; "there is
" of late a Commission made contrary to the said
" Commen Lawes unto certain persones the more
" parte whereof be Civilians not learned in the
" saide Lawes of this realme, autorising them to
" heare and determyne all matters and cawses
" exhibited into the saide Courte of Chauncery, by

" occasion whereof the matters there do daily more
" and more encrease . . . and by reason thereof
" there hath of late growne such a discorage unto
" the students of the said Commen Lawes, and the
" saide Commen Lawes have been of late so little
" estemed and had in experience, that fewe have
" or do regarde to take paynes of the profownde
" and sincere knolege of the same Lawe, by reason
" whereof there are now very fewe, and it is to be
" doubted that within fewe yeares there shall not
" be sufficient of lerned men within this realme to
" serve the King in that facultie." [1]   Apparently
the civilian drew business, and if the concluding
words of this wail from the Inns of Court are to be
taken seriously, the common law was in a bad way,
as we have the authority of Maitland for thinking
it was.   " In all directions," he says, speaking of it
under Henry VIII., " its province was being
" narrowed by the new courts, the Star Chamber,
" the Court of Requests, the Council of the North,
" and so forth.   There comes a moment when the
" stream of law reports which has been flowing
" ever since the time of Edward I. seems to be on
" the very point of running dry.   Reginald Pole,
" the highly educated young man, who is not far
" from the throne, is saying that the time has come
" for Roman Law: every well-intentioned nation
" is adopting it.   The Protector Somerset is
" keenly interested in getting a great civil law
" college founded at Cambridge." [2]

[1] " Acts of the Privy Council," N.S.   Vol. II., p. 48.
[2] " Collected Papers," Vol. III., p. 78.

The proposal to found a civil law college at Cambridge was put forward in 1549. It was to be called " Edward's College," and there is tacked on to this project, apparently as something separate, " a college of civilians to attend on the Council." [1] As regards Cambridge, there had that year been a visitation under Somerset's auspices the avowed object of which was to convert certain fellowships for the study of divinity into nests for civilians, and when Bishop Ridley told the Protector that to diminish the number of divines went against his conscience, Somerset reminded him how necessary the study of the Civil Law was " to all Treaties " with Foreign Princes and strangers, and how few " there be at this present to the King's Majesty's " service therein." [2]   So that only some three years after the students of the Inns of Court had complained to the Council that the inroads of the civil lawyers tended to bring about a shortage of practitioners at common law we find the Protector thus lamenting the lack of civilians for the diplomatic service.   The fact would seem to bear the construction that the latter were finding ample employment in the domestic courts—Chancery, Star Chamber, Requests, Faculties, and so forth.   As regards the presence of the civilians in the Court of Chancery, and elsewhere, the evidence of Sir Thomas Smith, writing, as he himself tells us, in the year 1565, is significant.   In his work " De Republica Anglorum," he describes the Chancellor

[1] S.P. Dom. (1547–1580), May, 1549.
[2] Burnet, Vol. II., Part 2, p. 222.

sitting on the left-hand side of Westminster Hall,
" accompanyed with the master of the Roules . . .
" and certain men learned in the civill lawe called
" Masters of the Chancerie—in latine they may be
" called Assessors." A few pages further on, after
alluding to the courts set up by Henry the Eighth,
" the one for the marches of Wales at Ludlow or
" elsewhere, another for the north parts of England
" at Yorke, where be many causes determined," he
adds that " these two courtes doe heare matters
" before them, part after the common law of
" Englande and part after the fashion of the
" Chancerie," which he has just said included a
civilian element.[1]

The usefulness of the civilian in foreign affairs
was a matter of course with the Tudor statesman ;
at a later date Bacon, though, as he says, he was of
the common law himself, did not fail to impress it
upon the future Duke of Buckingham. " I am so
" much a lover of Truth and of learning and of my
" Native Country," he wrote, " that I do heartily
" persuade that the Professors of that Law called
" Civilians (because the Civil Law is their guide)
" should not be discountenanced nor discouraged,
" else whensoever we shall have ought to do with
" any Foreign King or State, we shall be at a
" miserable loss for want of learned men in that
" profession." [2] To pass from the general to the
particular, it may be that a fillip was given to

---

[1] *Op. cit.*, pp. 52, 65, 66.
[2] " Mysteries of State and Government in Letters of Illustrious
Persons " (1691), p. 41.

Somerset's desire to have civilians at his elbow by
the dissatisfaction the French Ambassador was
expressing in 1550 with the English arrangements
for trying the cases of mutual depredations at sea.
The Council had already pointed out in a letter to
Sir John Mason, the English Ambassador in France,
that no higher court administering the civil law
existed in England than the Admiralty Court, for
which reason the cases in question had been assigned
to it.[1]   But the French Ambassador was not satis-
fied with its dignity ; he marvelled when admitted
to the presence of the Council why they had made
their judges inferior to the Admiralty, when the
French had made theirs of the Parliament above
the Admiralty ; and besides, there was an appeal
from the Admiralty Court, a circumstance incon-
sistent with the hearing of claims *summarie et de
plano*.[2]   Talk like this may have made the idea of a
higher tribunal administering the civil law seem
worth considering.   Incidentally it is to be noted
that it is assumed by both sides that the civil law
alone affords a basis for the settlement of such
international differences as the nations choose to
submit to the arbitrament of jurists.   " *In iis quae
" sola ratio commendat a iure Romano ad ius
" gentium tuta sit collectio.*" [3]

The founder of the College appears to have been
Dr. Richard Bodewell or Blodwell, who was Dean

[1] As mentioned, *supra*, p. 12, the international function of the
Admiralty Court was lucidly explained in this letter.   It is
set out by Froude, " Hist of England," IV., p. 540, note.
[2] " Acts of the Privy Council," N.S., Vol. III., pp. 163, 164.
[3] Bynkershoek, " Quaest. Iuris. Publici," c. 3.

of the Arches in 1511. The eighteenth century
antiquary, Dr. Andrew Ducarel, himself a civilian,
who contemplated publishing an account of
Doctors' Commons and made a collection of notes
to that end, says that at the beginning of the
Register of Members which goes back to that year,
Bodewell is described as " *huius collegii primus
presidens,*" and he credits him with forming the
original plan of association.[1] This may well have
been so ; but an evident allusion to the College in
a letter which Andrea Ammonio, Latin Secretary
to Henry VIII., addressed to Erasmus in 1511,
points to its being already well known by that time,
and therefore its foundation may be probably dated
a few years earlier. Ammonio is discussing the
subject of a suitable lodging in London for his
friend Erasmus. He dismisses the monastery where
he himself is living as out of the question, and then
adds : " *Circa aedem Pauli collegium est, ut nosti,*
" *quorundam doctorum quos aiunt laute vivere, ego*
" *puto in cloaca habitare.*" [2] Ammonio's contempt
for the residential amenities of the College does not
concern us so much as his revelation that the doctors
were already reputed to live there in some style,
and that Erasmus had heard of the confraternity.
It must therefore have been in existence for some
little time before this letter was written. The
name of Doctors' Commons it acquired before 1535,

[1] The MS., which is dated 1753, now belongs to the Incorporated Law Society.

[2] " Desiderii Erasmi Epistolae," cxxviii. Wolsey is said to
have planned the building of a fitting college in London for the
doctors.

as appears by a letter written from the College in
that year by the Dean of the Arches to Thomas
Cromwell.[1] We know from other sources that the
first home of the doctors in Paternoster Row was
not very commodious as compared with their subsequent one in Knightrider Street, provided for
them in 1568 by Dr. Henry Harvey, Master of
Trinity Hall and Dean of the Arches. Sir George
Buck, Master of the Revels under James the First,
published in 1615 " The Third Universitie of
" England, or a Treatise of the Foundations of all
" the Colledges . . . within and about this most
" famous cittie of London ; " and in dealing with " the
" Colledge of Civilians called Doctors' Commons," he
tells us that before it came into the street so long
associated with it the civilians were lodged in
Paternoster Row " in a meaner and lesser and less
" convenient house which was sometime a house for
" a prebendarie." In Buck's day and long afterwards
this house was a tavern known by the sign of the
Queen's Head. Buck, moreover, claims to have
been acquainted with Dr. Harvey, who obtained
the lease of Mountjoy Place or House for the
civilians ; " a reverend, learned and good man,"
he says, " whom I being a young scholler knew."
Harvey will be found described in many books as
the founder of the College. It adopted his coat of
arms and placed them in its dining hall with the
inscription, " *Huius Societatis Stator.*" The claim
of Dr. Bodewell to be its originator seems to have
been overlooked. He, however, belonged to the

[1] " Letters and Papers," Hen. VIII., Vol. IX., p. 181.

earlier era of the less convenient house ; and it
may be that, having come into possession of Mountjoy Place, the doctors, like other people who get on
in the world, discreetly forgot their humbler
address.

For Mountjoy House, the erstwhile town residence of the Blounts, William and Charles, fourth
and fifth Lords Mountjoy, the friends of Erasmus
and other scholars, had been called by Roger
Ascham " *domicilium Musarum.*" Not even that
tenancy, however, saved the place from having
fallen into decay by the middle of the century.
Perhaps the fact that Charles, who died in 1545, had
already diminished his patrimony, had something
to do with the disrepair of the building ; at any
rate, according to Ducarel, Dr. Harvey obtained a
lease of the premises, dated the 2nd February,
1567-8, from the Dean and Chapter of St. Paul's
to the Master, Fellows and Scholars of Trinity
Hall, Cambridge, " to be rebuilt by them for the
use of the Advocates and Doctors of the Arches,"
for the residue of an existing term and a further
one of ninety-nine years. In view of this arrangement it is not surprising that there were subsequent
squabbles between the civilians and the lessees as
to the right to grant chambers in the building.
The advocates were not themselves incorporated
until June 22nd, 1767, on which date they obtained
a charter and subsequently acquired the freehold.

Mr. Malden, the learned historian of Trinity Hall,
claims that Dr. Harvey made of Doctors' Commons

an off-shoot of that college.[1]   Harvey, we are told,
" was not content with establishing the position
" of his college in Cambridge. If it were to be
" worthy of its place as a training school for
" Civilians and Canonists, whose sphere of action
" extended into diplomacy and politics, or whose
" judicial abilities might be utilized in the Admir-
" alty Courts or in Diocesan Courts all over Eng-
" land, it must have some connexion with the
" world of London " ; and he adds with a natural
pride " no other College in Oxford or Cambridge
" ever attempted, I believe, to establish a society
" in London, as a voluntary college for the carrying
" out in practice in the great world of those studies
" which the College professed in the academic life."
Mr. Malden admits, however, that the organisation
of Doctors' Commons had already been begun
before Dr. Harvey took the matter up, and that in
a subsequent age the offspring quarrelled at great
length with its foster-mother at Cambridge. Into
the history of that litigation we need not go.

The advocates, from towards the close of Elizabeth's reign became a body composed entirely of
laymen and continued ever afterwards so constituted. This statement has been contradicted,
apparently because it was misunderstood to apply
to all civilians and not merely to civilians practising
as lawyers : there was never, of course, anything
to prevent a person holding a degree in the Civil
Law becoming a clergyman. But an attempt made
in 1807 to compel the Dean of the Arches to admit

[1] " Trinity Hall " (College Histories Series), p. 103, *et seq.*

a clergyman, Dr. Highmore, into the society of
Doctors' Commons was unsuccessful.[1] This was
a hard case, for the candidate, though in deacon's
orders, had dropped the clerical profession previously to going up to Cambridge for the special
purpose of qualifying himself for practice at
Doctors' Commons by taking a Doctor's degree.

Though the college of the English civilians was
thus fully established under Elizabeth, the courts
afterwards associated with Doctors' Commons were
not at once held there. The Arches still sat in
St. Mary-le-Bow ; the Court of Admiralty in
Southwark. The days when the doctors would
appear in their own college hall in scarlet robes
before the Dean, and, less resplendent in black gowns
before the Judge of the Admiralty, only came when
a new Doctors' Commons arose after the Fire of
London. It may be, however, of some interest to
note as marking the close connexion of the college
with the Universities, that in the Court of Arches
the advocates wore the hoods appropriate to their
degrees at Oxford or Cambridge " and all round,
black velvet caps." Even the proctors wore hoods
in this court, those of their degrees, if graduates ;
a hood " lined with lamb's skin " if they were not.[2]
Membership as an advocate was strictly confined

---

[1] The King *v.* The Archbishop of Canterbury (Highmore's
Case), 8 East, 213.

[2] See Chamberlayne, " Angliae Notitia," as to the seventeenth
century ; and Floyer, " The Proctor's Practice," as to the
eighteenth.

at a later date to graduates of the two Universities :
one John Hawkesworth, upon whom in the
eighteenth century a Lambeth degree of LL.D. had
been conferred, in vain sought admission.[1]

A peculiarity of the college, which for comparative purposes perhaps deserves further
investigation, was that its members were surro-
gates of the Judge of the Admiralty Court, and
could lawfully act for him in his absence.[2] Sir
Travers Twiss, in stating this, goes a long way back
for a parallel, to the fourteenth-century " Order of
the Courts of the Consuls of the Sea " at Valencia,
where it was the practice both of the Consuls and
of the Appeal Judge to delegate their offices to
members of the Guild of Navigators in a case of
necessity. It is, at any rate, certain that the
Judge of the Admiralty Court often sat by deputy
in Henry the Eighth's time ; Dr. Husse is sitting
for Dr. Tregonwell in 1536, Dr. Trevor for Dr.
Husse in 1542, and Dr. Jeffery for Dr. Leyson in
1547.[3] Mr. Marsden says the deputy received his
appointment from the Admiral; and a manuscript
list of the Judges of the Admiralty Court amongst
Sir Julius Caesar's papers in the British Museum
has a note that in the time of Dr. Lewis (1558–1584)
the Queen joined several Doctors in commission
with him for his assistants in piracy cases.[4] Such
appointments seem unnecessary if Sir Travers

[1] Irving, " Introduction to the Study of the Civil Law," citing
Kenrick's Poems (1768), p. 168.
[2] " Black Book of the Admiralty," Vol. IV., p. 459.
[3] " Select Pleas in the Court of Admiralty." Vol. I. p. lx.
[4] Add. MSS., 30222.

Twiss is to be taken literally : but possibly his statement indicates the theory only. On the other hand, Dr. Lewis has left it on record that he practised as an advocate for five or six years after he became Judge in 1558, " so as to make a competent living thereby " ; and apparently Sir William Petre and Dr. Wotton were qualified to sit for him when he had a brief, for he complains that when they began to withdraw themselves from the Court he was compelled to attend to his judicial duties and forego his advocacy.[1]

We may wind up our survey of the doctors in Tudor times with a pleasant fact or two, touching their collegiate habits, derived from their own records. Every day in term time a portion of the Holy Scriptures was read in the Latin tongue during dinner: and in 1575, at Burghley's suggestion, the privilege was granted to the Society of importing wine free of duty for the use of their common table. It is gratifying to find from an examination of the dates given that it was five years before this economic advantage accrued to the College of Advocates that they excluded their merely honorary members (who had become too numerous) from their commons.[2] That the sequence of events is not otherwise redounds to the credit both of the honorary members and of the College.

---

[1] Stow, " Survey of London," 1753 ed., Vol. I., Book I., Chap. XII. S.P. Dom. Eliz., Vol. CVI., 60.

[2] Oughton, " Ordo Iudiciorum," Chap. I. " De Hospitio Dominorum Advocatorum."

There is not wanting evidence, however, that the professional prospects of the civilians which seemed to be a-ripening under Edward the Sixth were nipped in the bud whilst yet Elizabeth reigned. When the middle of the century was past the common law began to pick itself up. The second dedication of Richard Crompton's book on the Jurisdiction of Courts, published in 1594, shows, for example, at once a pride in the common law and *esprit de corps* amongst its practitioners—" *As* " *touts mes Companions del Middle Temple* " *Richard Crompton desire l'encrease de science in* " *les Comon leyes de cet Realme.*" Coke has recorded with a sneer and evident satisfaction the decline at this period of those " divers under-courts to hear complaints by bill of poor people " which owed their origin to Cardinal Wolsey and were manned by civilians and canonists. " One," he says, " kept in Whitehall, the other before the " King's Almoner Dr. Stokesley, a man that had " more learning than discretion to be a judge : " a third sat in the Lord Treasurer's Chamber be- " side the Star Chamber, and the fourth at the " Rolls in the afternoon. These Courts were " greatly haunted for a time . . . but then every " man was weary of them and resorted to the " common law." [1] As regards the civilians in the Admiralty Court there is the pathetic complaint of the judge, Dr. Lewis, as to the state of business there, a reference to which has already been made. He has no fixed salary : his share of the goods and

[1] " Reports," Part 3., Preface.

chattels of attainted pirates is gone, for the Admiral
has transferred the right thereto to the Crown :
worse still, the Queen's Bench has " terrified " the
suitors by prohibitions grounded on specious
fictions : and finally, the Queen has granted to the
Company of Merchants trading with Spain and
Portugal, upon whose business the Court of Admiralty " stood chiefly," a right to hear and determine
their own litigation. Already in 1558 there had
been a case where London merchants had been
deemed the fittest arbitrators in a commercial
dispute, over the heads, so to speak, of both the
Chief Justice of the Queen's Bench and the Judge
of the Admiralty Court. In this suit of Wynthrop
v. Combes the first-named judge had issued an
attachment against the judge in Admiralty for
intermeddling in his jurisdiction : both dignataries
were heard before the Council, who endeavoured to
arrange a *modus vivendi ;* but ultimately the Council
sent a letter to Alderman Marten and four other
London merchants authorising them to call Wyn-
tropp and Combes before them and " to hear and
determine all matters of controversy between
them." [1] And in or about the year 1570 we find
the Lord Mayor and Sheriffs of London (either
moved by the result of such a case as the foregoing
or by the success of the fiction practised in the
Common Law Courts alleging the good ship *Tiger*
to have arrived in Cheapside) [2] trying their hands

[1] " Acts of the Privy Council," N.S. Vol. VII., p. 62.
[2] See Ridley's " View of the Civil Law " 1676 ed., p. 172.

at stealing a march upon the jurisdiction of the Admiralty Court : in this instance, however, the usurpers are reproved by the Queen and commanded to intermeddle in no such matters.[1] But it is worth notice in connexion with the City's tendencies that in the constitution of the court set up by statute in 1601 for dealing with causes arising out of policies of assurance, " eight grave and discreet merchants " were added to three civilians, including the Judge of the Admiralty Court, and three common lawyers, including the Recorder.[2] This Act of Parliament seems to have long rankled in the minds of the civilians. Dr. Robert Wiseman reverts to it in the plea on behalf of the civilians' profession he put forward in 1656, and sadly points to the small number of the learned appointed to the tribunal devised to carry it out compared with this intolerable deal of merchants. " Let them keep within their own sphere," he observes, and proceeds to draw a fancy picture of merchants rashly promoted to dispense justice in the Court of Admiralty, where he is sure they would not be fair to their employés the mariners.[3] Nor was it alone in the mercantile field that the frost attacked the activities of the doctors of the civil law. The celebrated Dr. Duck, writing in the next generation, has recorded with a bitter humour that " in the latter end of her (Elizabeth's) reign, " her chief Ministers chose rather to use an Amanu-

---

[1] S.P. Dom.   May 20, 1570.
[2] 43 Eliz., cap. 12.
[3] " The Excellency of the Civil Law," p. 148.

" ensis in transcribing Leagues and Contracts than
" the Assistance of skilful Civilians . . . having,
" perhaps, fallen upon that ancient caution in
" relation to wills, ' *A testamento dolus malus et*
" *iuris consultus abesto*.' " [1]

[1] " Use and Authority of the Civil Law in England." 1724 ed.,
p. xxxviii.

V. THE LATTER DAYS OF THE CIVILIANS

James the First brought with him from Scotland a liking for the Civil Law. He said that "if it should be taken away it would make an Entry into Barbarism," meaning that there would be no international law left.[1] Much might be written on the text of this antithesis, not without very modern illustrations : but in truth James was only emphasising the international aspect of the Roman law in order to allay the fears of those who saw him favouring its professors within the realm. It may be, however, that the civilians in England read into such royal pronouncements a possibility of a new era for them. In 1607 Sir Thomas Ridley dedicated to James his " View of the Civil Law," a work designed to show the needlessness of the common lawyer's jealousy. We have already met with more than one symptom of that antagonism, notably in the complaint of the students of the Inns of Court in Edward the Sixth's time touching the encroachments of the civilian practitioners. In the fifty years between then and the accession of James, time had done much to diminish the causes

---

[1] Wynne's " Life of Jenkins," 1, p. lxxxiv.

of the common lawyer's anxiety : broadminded
men thought the rivalry a mere schism that ought
to be cured. Dr. John Cowell, Master of Trinity
Hall and Regius Professor of the Civil Law at
Cambridge, in the " Institutiones Iuris Anglicani,"
which he published in 1605, had deplored the
inveteratae simultates, quas iam diu legum Angli-
carum professores et iuris imperatorii in hoc regno
invicem exercuerunt : and his design two years
later, in putting forth the law-dictionary called
" The Interpreter," a book of which we shall have
more to say, seems largely to have been to mediate
between the two professions by exhibiting the
common elements in their respective studies. The
versatile William Fulbecke of Gray's Inn, in his
" Parallele of the Civill Law, the Canon Law and
the Common Law," published in 1601, had taken
much the same line, so that it may be said that in
the early years of the seventeenth century an olive
branch was held up on either side. " It seemed
" strange unto me," wrote Fulbecke, " that these
" three laws should not, as the three Graces, have
" their hands linked together and their lookes
" directly fixed the one upon the other, but like
" the two faces of Janus the one should be turned
" from the other."

Unfortunately a comprehensive idealism such a
Fulbecke's stood no chance when Coke came upon
the scene. There was again added to what, on the
surface at least, had been only a professional rivalry,
the rancour of politics. It chanced that in the
year 1607 Dr. Cowell had been inspired by the

example of one Calvinus of Heidelburg to compile his famous " Interpreter." It was certainly a book in which the supporters of kingly absolutism might find a text or two to their taste, although to read its modest preface one can hardly imagine that any motive other than a desire for academic fame had prompted its production. " My true " ende," declared the author, " is the advancement " of knowledge : I shall think my paines sufficiently " recompensed if they may be found but worthy " to stirre up one learned man to amend mine " errours." The learned man who was stirred up to amend the doctor's errors, though in a sense very different from his expectation, was the Chief Justice of the Common Pleas, Sir Edward Coke.

A considerable period elapsed before this happened—an interval not without its significance. Meanwhile in 1609 had occurred the well-known wordy encounters between the King and Coke touching the Royal Prerogative, wherein the Chief Justice may not have come off with such flying colours as the posthumous Part XII. of his Reports would lead us to suppose.[1] There are circumstances in the story of the prosecution of Cowell and the suppression of his book (ostensibly at the instigation of the Parliament on constitutional grounds) from which it might be argued that Coke, who was undoubtedly at the back of those proceedings, made the Professor into a kind of whipping-boy for his Majesty. The old contest between

[1] See *Eng. Hist. Rev.*, Vol. XVIII., p. 664, " James I. and Sir Edward Coke," by Roland G. Usher.

common lawyer and civilian was linked by Coke with controversies of much wider import, though ostensibly it remained one as to the excellence of their respective systems and the proper boundaries of their practice. Dr. Cowell, somewhat gratuitously, it is true, had included in " The Interpreter " a quotation from the French civilian, Hotman, reflecting in severe terms upon Littleton's " Tenures." The Frenchman had dared to describe Littleton's work—Coke's Littleton—as *incondite, absurde et inconcinne scriptum*. " It is a desperate and " dangerous matter," we read in one of Coke's prefaces to The Reports, " for civilians and " canonists (I speak what I know and not without " just cause) to write either of the common laws " of England which they profess not, or against " them which they know not." When we read the Proclamation suppressing Dr. Cowell's " Interpreter " in 1610 and find one of the grounds for the action taken is stated to be " speaking irreverently " of the Common Law of England and the works " of some of the most famous and ancient Judges " therein," we with difficulty resist the conclusion that Cowell's attack at secondhand upon Coke's idol weighed with his lordship not much less than the Professor's unconstitutional theory of Kingship. There was another reason besides " The Interpreter " why the downfall of Dr. Cowell would be acceptable to the Chief Justice as involving indirectly in its censure other more highly placed persons. Cowell had been the draughtsman of the *Articuli Cleri* for his patron the Archbishop

Bancroft, in furtherance of that prelate's struggle
for a wider ecclesiastical jurisdiction in despite of
the common law : and, moreover, it was the
Archbishop who had egged on James in his quaint
desire to sit as judge in the King's Bench. Coke
successfully thwarted that particular ambition :
but in passing we may note that according to the
Venetian Ambassador, writing home to his government in August, 1609, James came one day into
the High Court of Admiralty " at the reading of
" the cases, and to the amazement of everyone,
" summed up the evidence of all the witnesses."
In view of Coke's prohibition and his dislike both
of the Admiralty Court and of the civilians who
practised before it, there is a peculiar piquancy in
this escapade of the British Solomon. As to " The
Interpreter " itself, as soon as Parliament was
moved to take exception to it, nearly three years
after its publication, James professed to repudiate
its author. He had already learnedly explained
his notion of the scope of the civil law within the
realm in a speech to the Houses.[1] That he really
was prepared to protect the civilians so far as he
could appears from an episode that occurred
during the previous year. The King was discussing with the Judges the complaints of the
doctors practising in admiralty as to the curtail-
ment of their business by writs of prohibition.
These complaints, with the answers of the Judges
thereto, were afterwards set out by Coke in the

[1] Wilson, " Life and Reign of King James the First " (1653).
p. 47.

Fourth Part of his Institutes,[1] the replies forming the argument from the common law side, supported by many supposed authorities : but as Mr. Justice Buller remarked in the eighteenth century, " that part of Coke's work has been " always received with great caution and frequently " contradicted." " He " says Buller, " seems to have " entertained not only a jealousy of, but an enmity " against, that (the admiralty) jurisdiction." [2] What is related of Coke's behaviour at the meeting when these *Articuli Admiralitatis* were being discussed, bears out, if the chronicler may be believed, the conclusion that Buller had arrived at regarding Coke's dislike of the civilian merely as such. He appears upon this occasion to have attacked Sir Thomas Crompton, the successor of Dale in the Admiralty judgeship, for no other assignable reason than that he was a person of eminence in his profession. The Lord Chief Justice provoked James to retort that Crompton was as good a man as he.[3] Crompton is described in the State Papers of the time as a man of great learning in the civil law.[4] He had been Advocate-General under Elizabeth and was Chancellor of the diocese of London and Member for Oxford : but, " in truth," as Buller adds in the case already cited, " my Lord Coke could not bear anything connected with the Civil Law." In such an atmosphere did the civilian lawyers in

---

[2] " Institutes," IV., p. 135.
[2] In Smart *v.* Wolff (1789), 3 T.R. at p. 348.
[3] Lodge, " Illustrations of English History," Vol. III., p. 364.
[4] S.P. Dom. Addenda, James I. May 29, 1608.

England begin the seventeenth century. To show something of the share that James and Coke between them had in creating it enables us the better to understand the civilian's position forty years later.

With this introduction it may be said that as a body the lawyers at Doctors' Commons were passively rather than actively involved in the political strife of the succeeding reign. The strife itself was inevitable. The Tudors had wielded powers greater than those possessed by any former English sovereigns. In their time the powers had been necessary, but in the next age the prerogative of the Crown, no longer employed in strengthening and maintaining the national unity, needed to be curtailed. It was in a somewhat similar fashion that the Court of Star Chamber, the name of which became a byword, had started by being a useful and beneficent tribunal. The process by which the checking of the prerogative was accomplished, through civil war and the experiment of a republic resting upon the power of the Puritan sword, has been described by many historians according to their several predilections, and needs no further comment. But it may be mentioned that it had been during the Tudor period that the civilians in England had, so to speak, attained their majority, and that it was probably only natural that they would be exposed to the prejudice of the popular party when it in turn grew up. As professors of the Roman Law they were associated with an imperialistic system. They were all advocates in the Court of Arches, and in the seventeenth century the Bishops were regarded as the heads of an institution that was necessarily in alliance with the King. These facts would be reason good enough for popular suspicion. The ill-omened maxim, *Quod placuit principi*, was still upon occasion dragged from its seclusion as a testimony against those in whose books it lurked, although what was pleasing to the Prince was by no means always pleasing to individual civilians. Charles' order, for example, that goods taken out of French prizes should be sold without waiting for the sentence of the Admiralty Court was keenly resented by Sir Henry Marten the judge. As regards the civilians and the Church, they were sometimes far from seeing eye to eye with Laud in matters of ecclesiastical jurisdiction. But undoubtedly marks of the royal favour were bestowed upon them by the first two Stuarts, less, as it seems, in response to any seeking than because the Crown took the support of their profession for granted. Under Elizabeth they had been addressed officially as " Her Majesty's right trusty friends " : the assumption was still made. In 1634 the College of Advocates was expressly exempted from the ship-money tax imposed upon the City, and it appears from a letter written by Secretary Windebank to Sir Henry Marten that the King specially notified his departure for York " for the defence of this Kingdom " not only to the Judge of the Admiralty Court but to the whole Society of Doctors' Commons. " You are to think," Marten is told,

" of come considerable assistance." [1]   He was, as
already stated, quite capable of taking an independent view of Charles' proceedings, but efforts to
" nobble " learned bodies in the interest of some
particular policy of state are not even yet unknown.
Mr. Malden, in his history of Trinity Hall, is inclined to wonder that the doctors did not receive
a charter of incorporation from either James I.
or Charles I. The fact that the existing corporation of Trinity Hall was already in possession of
Doctors' Commons as lessees might partly explain
the omission, but there is a further and quite
different reason in the various " politics " of the
doctors themselves. When the civil war came we
find some of them on both sides. The eminent
Dr. Duck was a close adherent of Charles, who,
when a prisoner in the Isle of Wight, would fain
have obtained his advice in negotiating with the
Parliament. The successor of Sir Henry Marten
in the Admiralty Court, Dr. Richard Zouche,
though a royalist in the war, was enough in favour
with Cromwell to be included in the commission [2]
appointed to try the case of Don Pantaleon Sa in
1653, though he had before then been deprived of
his judgeship. On the other hand, Dr. Godolphin
appointed with others to fill the place of Zouche,
was on the Puritan side, and the name of Dr. Isaac
Dorislaus, on whose behalf Cromwell wrote to
Trinity Hall to secure the succession to Duck's

[1] S.P. Dom. Feb. 12, 1638/9.

[2] This special commission of oyer and terminer included, besides
Zouche, two or three other civilians.   It sat in Westminster Hall.
Cobbett's " State Trials," Vol. V.

chambers for him, is amongst those of the regicides. A Dutchman, though as Fuller puts it, " very much Anglized in language and behaviour," Dorislaus was a republican who had previously given offence to the Court by a lecture delivered from the Chair of History at Cambridge.[1] Not all the doctors, then, were upholders of a Byzantine theory of the State.

Leaving the threadbare controversies of that time, we may now gather from scattered entries in the State Papers something of the professional life of the lawyers at Doctors' Commons during the first half of the seventeenth century. We ought not to omit all reference to the appearance of Albericus Gentilis in the Admiralty Court as the standing advocate on behalf of the Spanish Embassy, from 1605 until his death in 1608 : although it seems that Gentilis was never admitted a member of the College of Advocates. His notes of cases made during that employment were published by his brother Scipio in 1613 under the title of " Hispanicae Advocationis, in quo tractatu diversae quaestiones maritimae perlustruntur et deciduntur. Libri duo." Probably Gentilis, as Professor of Civil Law at Oxford and a member of Gray's Inn was accounted an honorary member of Doctors' Commons.

Much business was soon afterwards being transacted there, both in the Dining Hall, and in chambers. In 1629 the King having referred

[1] Fuller's " Hist. of the University of Cambridge " (1840 ed.) p. 313.

a petition to Sir Henry Marten, he " appoints the morrow at 3 of the clock at his chambers " for examination of its truth and settling the matter in difference ; [1] and other instances might be given. In 1635/6 twenty-eight civilians— practically the whole college—are consulted upon a point of prize law. A vessel laden with tobacco had been captured by a Dunkirker and condemned in the prize-court at Dunkirk and afterwards on appeal at Brussels on the ground that tobacco was victuals. The " Doctors of the Civil Law, Judges and Advocates of the Court of Arches," as they are styled in the reference, report that in their opinion these sentences are neither justified by the Law of Nations nor by the treaty of 1630 between England and Spain.[2] In July, 1636, Dr. Duck advises as to the Archbishop's right of visitation of the Universities.[3] In the following February a petition to Laud is referred to Duck and Sir John Lambe, who appoint a day to hear the cause in the Dining Room.[4] There is frequent mention during the next few years of the use of the Dining Room as a court. The College would seem to have taken its vacation early : on the 14th July, 1636, Duck writes to Lambe that " all of Doctors' Commons are out of town." A good deal of pre- liminary work is sent to the doctors in ecclesiastical cases. Lambe is enjoined by the Archbishop to

[1] S.P. Dom. May 19, 1629.
[2] S.P. Dom. Feb. 3, 1635/6.
[3] S.P. Dom. July, 1636, *passim*.
[4] S.P. Dom. Feb. 23, 1636/7.

patch up a matrimonial difference " in a peaceable
manner if he can or else that the husband answer
in the High Commission." [1] In June, 1638, the
case of Mr. Pinson, accused of " inconformity "
to the Church of England, because (*inter alia*) his
wife had gone to be churched without a veil, is sent
for hearing in the Dining Room before Sir John
Lambe and Sir Charles Caesar.[2] The latter was
the son of Sir Julius, and is described by a contemporary observer as a " woodcock " and a " very
ass." [3] His remarks upon the behaviour of Mrs.
Pinson, who had contumaciously placed a table-
napkin upon her head when the parson pointed out
her omission, have unfortunately not been recorded. In 1640 the petition of a printer to Bishop
Juxon touching the re-printing of the book, " Re-
formatio Legum Ecclesiasticarum," by unlicensed
persons, is sent to Lambe " to settle the difference,
or certify where he conceives the right to be." [4]
These extracts will suffice to show the variety of
the business disposed of at this time by the civilians
at Doctors' Commons. The Court of Admiralty,
though it also was manned by them, was not yet
held there.

Some effort appears to have been made in the
reign of Charles the First to find places for the
civilian lawyer in the provinces. Wiseman, writing
about 1656, says, " If we look back no further than

[1] S.P. Dom. Mar. 17, 1637/8.
[2] S.P. Dom. June 11, 1638.
[3] S.P. Dom. Mar. 28, 1639.
[4] S.P. Dom. June 27, 1640.

" twenty years we shall remember the Civil Law
" did so far spread itself up and down this nation
" that there was not any one county which had
" not some part of the government thereof managed
" and exercised by one or more of that profession." [1]
It is to be remembered that he was engaged in
making out a case for the Civil Law : he makes
this assertion the ground for observing that it was
" naturalized " and " not to be reputed or looked
upon by us a stranger any longer." When we do
look back twenty years from 1656 we find that
there was an Order of a Committee of both Houses
in 1635 whereby the judge of a Vice-Admiral of
the Coast was to be a discreet and learned man in
the civil law dwelling or resorting within the circuit
of his office, or, for want of a civilian, one learned
in the common laws. It also appears from a
charter of 1640 granted to the town of Southampton
that a civil lawyer " might " be added to the Mayor
and Recorder sitting as judges in the admiralty
court of local jurisdiction. But even if civilian
deputies were appointed in all the nineteen dis-
tricts which boasted Vice-Admirals and even if all
the other boroughs having, like Southampton, a
local admiralty—there were less than twenty such
towns—chose to bring in a civilian to help them,
it would not have amounted to very much. It is
difficult, however, to see to what else Wiseman was
alluding when he speaks of civilians exercising
their profession in every county if not to such
provisions on their behalf as we have mentioned :

[1] " The Excellency of the Civil Law," p. 180.

and it is to be noted that he speaks in the past
tense as though the civilians' ubiquity, if indeed
it was ever established, had been shortlived.

Cromwell kept a tight hand upon the College.
His polite letter to Trinity Hall, written within
two days of the royalist Doctor Duck's decease,
with the object of securing for the republican
Dorislaus the dead man's chambers at Doctors'
Commons, has another significance besides that of
showing that the lettings were controlled from
Cambridge. As to the Admiralty Court, it went in
fear of the Council of State : but as, about the same
time, the Chief Justice of the King's Bench had to
choose between resigning his seat and forfeiting his
independence, there is nothing surprising in the
subservience of the lesser court.   There are several
letters from the Admiralty Judges seeking the
instructions of the Council as to the decision of
causes before them.   They write to Cromwell from
Doctors' Commons in 1654, " we have long waited
" an order on the case of Palache on a report to the
" Council, and his proctor pressing for judgment we
" remind you thereof and certify that if we receive
" no order to the contrary we shall let the case go
" to hearing." [1]   This attitude was further secured
by the appointment of judges in admiralty sometimes for a few months only.   Dr. Godolphin, Dr.
Clark, and a barrister named Cocke, are appointed
by an Act of July 30th, 1653, until March 25th,
1654, " and no longer."   Godolphin and Cocke are
again appointed on May 19th, 1659, until June

[1] S.P. Dom. Dec. 5, 1654. See also *ibid.* Oct. 27, 1653.

H

30th, 1659, "and no longer": and again on July
19th until the following December. The mention
of Cocke reminds us that the ancient monopoly
of the civilians is being encroached upon : although
a common lawyer he was not only made an admiralty judge but sat also in the Prerogative Court.[1]
In 1649 one Stevens, a member of the House of
Commons and a common lawyer, was made a judge
in Admiralty : "for which place," says Whitelock,
"he was not very fit."[2] This leavening of Doctors'
Commons was probably meant to be disciplinary :
but, as we know, times of unrest are ever the opportunity of the unqualified.

On the other hand, the jurisdiction of the
Admiralty Court was settled by various Acts and
Ordinances during the Interregnum, and the interference of the common law courts by way of prohibition was for the time being staved off. Mr.
Marsden tells us the business of the Court increased
during this period, and that probably the reason
why the attack of the common lawyers began
afresh after the Restoration was "the disfavour
which then attached to all the doings of the
Commonwealth, including the recent settlement of
Admiralty jurisdiction."[3]

There can be little doubt that with the passing
away of the Star Chamber, the Court of Requests
and other tribunals of Tudor origin, the Court of
Admiralty, which for historical reasons had always
been the most natural field for the civilians' prac-

[1] Coote's "Civilians."
[2] "Memorials," p. 405.
[3] "Select Pleas," Vol. II., p. lxxix.

tice, became their mainstay. It is clear from the
manner in which the famous argument of Sir
Leoline Jenkins, on behalf of the Bill before the
Lords in 1660 to ascertain the jurisdiction of the
Admiralty, diverges into a plea for the usefulness
of the civilians' profession, that he considered the
continuance of the latter closely if not chiefly bound
up with the business of the Admiralty Court.   The
Bill, which embodied the provisions of a Commonwealth Ordinance of 1648, was thrown-out by
Parliament : and with the growth of commercial
law at Westminster under such a judge as Holt
towards the end of the century the Court was
bound to diminish in importance.   Even with the
ecclesiastical business thrown in, the civilian had
difficulty in maintaining his footing.   " Although "
says Fuller, writing in the year 1655, " the civilians
" kept canon law *in commendam* with their own
" profession, yet both twisted together are scarce
" strong enough (especially in our own sad days)
" to draw to them a liberal livelihood." [1]   Things
were no better after 1660.

The Restoration was followed by two national
calamities, both of which affected the home of the
civilians.   In 1665 came the Plague, which was
particularly bad in the neighbourhood of Doctors'
Commons.[2]   In September of that year, in consequence of this epidemic, the King addressed a
letter to the Mayor and Aldermen of Oxford re-
questing them to give " a free and fair reception "

[1] " Hist. of the University of Cambridge " (1840 ed.), p. 225.
[2] S.P. Dom.   Nov.? 1665.

to the judges and other officers of the Admiralty
Court, now ordered to be kept in the Common Hall
of that city.[1]   It had lately been held in part of
the disused Church of St. Margaret-at-Hill in the
borough of Southwark.[2]   At Oxford, according to
some authorities, it sat in the Hall of Jesus College,
of which the Judge, Sir Leoline Jenkins, was a
Fellow ; but as its excursion thither extended
only to a few months it does not greatly matter
whether the municipality or the university gave
it house-room.   It is of somewhat more interest to
know that the Court of Admiralty moved into
Doctors' Commons early in 1666 for the first time
in its history, and was thenceforth to be held in
the Hall of that building, as appears from a warrant
to Jenkins dated in January.[3]

Unfortunately the Hall and the rest of the original Doctors' Commons perished in the Great Fire
of the following September.   The civilians, again
exiled, then held their courts at Exeter House in
the Strand until 1672, by which time their college
had been rebuilt [4] and in February, 1673, we find
" the Society of Doctors' Commons " petitioning
that their ancient freedoms and immunities might
be preserved and confirmed to them.[5]   Sir Leoline
Jenkins was instrumental at this time in procuring
their freedom from several taxes and assessments

---

[1] S.P. Dom. Sept. 15, 1665.
[2] Pepys' " Diary," Mar. 17, 1663.
[3] S.P. Dom. Jan. 25, 1666. Coote (" Civilians ") is mis-
leading on this point.
[4] Coote's " Civilians."
[5] S.P. Dom. Feb. 1, 1673. " Entry Book," 37, p. 54.

which his biographer says had been unduly laid
on them by the Court of Aldermen; and afterwards, in 1682, when Secretary of State, he obtained for them " exemption from all Ward and
" Parish Offices, in the same manner as Serjeants,
" Council (*sic*) and Attorneys of the King's
" Temporal Courts." [1]

The college then re-erected was that which the
civilians inhabited until the end. Something of its
architectural aspect may be gleaned from a drawing
of its " Great Quadrangle," made when the building
was on the eve of demolition in the last century,
which is preserved in the London Museum.
Judging by this, its appearance differed little from
still existing seventeenth-century aggregations of
chambers in the Temple and elsewhere. The
larger quadrangle was entered by an archway from
Knightrider Street, and opposite to this entrance
was another archway leading into a second quadrangle and a garden. The building included,
besides the houses in which the advocates resided
or had chambers, the Common Hall and Dining
Room, of which we have already heard, and a
Library.[2] The Library, which was over the
Dining Room, has been called " spacious and well
stocked." [3] Every bishop at his consecration was
supposed to subscribe a sum for the purchase of
books, and there were other benefactors. The
books were dispersed in 1861.

[1] Wynne's " Life of Jenkins," Vol. I., p. liii.
[2] See " Doctors' Commons: Its Courts and Registries," by
G. J. Foster (1868), p. 5.
[3] Noorthouck's " Hist. of London " (1773), p. 584.

Great Britain found herself at war again with Holland in 1672, and early in the following year two spies named Zas and Arton were caught in England. The commission to try them included, besides Colonel John Russell and ten other military officers, four doctors of the civil law, of whom Jenkins was one. It had been drafted by Sir Robert Wiseman, the Advocate-General, and Sir Walter Walker, D.C.L., and approved by the King. Military law was, of course, from old time within the civilians' province : but the inquisitorial mode of trial here proposed to be adopted is not without interest. The commission, which is dated February 24th, 1673, recites that Zas and Arton are charged with coming over to act as spies, and empowers the judges " by such just and lawful means and even " by pains to be inflicted, if otherwise he or they " refuse (so as the said pains be not extended to " the laming disjointing or dismembering of his " or their bodies) to compel them to answer to " such interrogatories for discovering the design " they came over about . . . as may be exhibited " by Sir R. Wiseman and Sir W. Walker, the King's " Counsel, and to pass sentence upon them, pro- " vided that no sentence of death be put in execu- " tion without the King's further order." [1] It has been suggested that there was a sinister connexion between the use of torture in England in order to obtain evidence and the civil law. The practice, though unknown to the common law, was never-

[1] S.P. Dom. Oct., 1672–Feb., 1673, pp. 557, 605.

theless long established in the administration of the
ordinary criminal law, and the presence of a civilian
at an examination by " pains to be inflicted "
seems to have been considered necessary, probably
in order that the rules prescribed by the civil law
should be duly observed.[1]   The case just mentioned
did not arise in the course of the ordinary criminal
law : but it is of somewhat later date than the
period which, according to Mr. Jardine, saw the
end of torture in England, and the management of
the examination was evidently in the hands of the
two civilians named.

The Revolution of 1688 found the civilians
divided in their opinions, as the Civil War had done.
When Dr. William Oldys, the Admiralty Advocate,
was deprived of his office in 1693 for refusing to
prosecute as pirates persons holding letters of
marque from James the Second, Dr. Littleton was
quite ready to take his place. When Oldys was
examined as to his reasons by a Committee of the
Privy Council, Dr. Pinfold concurred in his opinion,
whilst Littleton's contention that the King by his
abdication had ceased to have power to grant such
commissions was supported by Dr. Matthew Tindal,
who wrote a pamphlet setting forth the whole
controversy.[2]

[1] Jardine, " A Reading on the Use of Torture in the Criminal
Law of England " (1837), p. 64.

[2] " An essay concerning the Laws of Nations and the Rights of
Sovereigns, with an account of what was said at the Council
Board by the Civilians upon the question whether their Majesties'
subjects taken at sea, acting by the late King's commission, might
not be looked upon as pirates. With reflections upon the
arguments of Sir T. P. and Dr. Ol . . ." 1694.

From the date of the rebuilding after the Fire, the College of Advocates had still nearly 200 years of institutional life : but even before the close of the seventeenth century there are signs that the profession of the civil law is tending to become an anachronism. The lamentations of Dr. Lewis under Elizabeth, of Dr. Duck under Charles the First, and the testimony of Fuller in his day, as to the waning employments and emoluments of the civil lawyers, are repeated in the year 1695 by another writer who calls himself Solon Secundus. " The Civil Law is in vogue with the Dutch," he complains, " and indeed with the greatest part of " Europe, England excepted, where 'tis run down " and our Common Law advanced above it : " t'other is cramped and scrubbed and whipt into " a corner, and impeded mightily in its Progress " and Practice." [1] The date at which this last *vox clamantis* is raised seems to show a curious in-advertence on the part of its owner as to the trend of English affairs. There had been a period—not a particularly short one—round about the beginning of the seventeenth century when the admiralty lawyers at Doctors' Commons had been ahead of the Common Law Courts in the development of commercial law, but the latter had by now caught them up. From the time of Lord Chief Justice Holt the general mercantile business of the country had tended more and more to be absorbed by the ordinary courts of law, which, without admitting

[1] " Solon Secundus : or Some Defects in the English Laws," p. 17.

it, would take a leaf or two out of the civilians'
Roman book, and draw upon both the " law of
nature " and what Selden had called the " Justinian " law for guidance. There is already discernible that *rapprochement* between the Court of
King's Bench and the Civil Law (where it can be
serviceable) that had become a matter of course by
the time of Mansfield a century later : and it is
important to notice it inasmuch as the more
perfect it became the less need there would be for
the separate professional existence of the civilian,
so far as mercantile law was concerned.

But the " cornering " of the civilian, if we may
adopt the phrase of Solon Secundus, was not only
effected through the inevitable advance of the
common law in mercantile matters. Even the
sacred province of the public Law of Nations, once
his undisputed monopoly, he had now to share with
the Judges and the Law Officers of the Crown. An
opinion as to the power of the Crown to affect by
treaty the right of English subjects to claim their
goods out of prizes brought into England by a
foreign captor, given in 1689, is signed by Holt,
by Pollexfen J., and the Attorney and Solicitor-
General, as well as by Sir Charles Hedges, the
Judge of the Admiralty Court and Doctor Pinfold.[1]
This practice is well established by the middle of
the next century. An opinion taken in 1744 as to
the power of the Crown to distribute prizes between
Dutch and English joint-captors is signed not only

[1] " Law and Custom of the Sea " (Navy Records Society).
Vol. II., p. 124.

by two civilians, Doctor Paul and Doctor Strahan,
but by Sir Dudley Ryder and Sir William Murray,
afterwards Lord Mansfield.[1] The famous " *réponse
sans réplique* " to the King of Prussia in 1753,
arising out of the matter of the Silesian Loan,
dealt, as is well known, with the nature and extent
of the jurisdiction over the ships and cargoes of
neutrals, a topic purely of international law. It
is signed by two civilians, Sir George Lee, Dean of
the Arches, and Doctor Paul, Advocate-General, but
also by Ryder, the Attorney, and Sir William
Murray, the Solicitor-General. Sir Robert Phillimore says that this document was largely the work
of Lee : on the other hand, we are told in the
Preface to Hay and Marriot's Reports that the
future Lord Mansfield, " from the place of his birth
" had a predilection for the imperial or civil law "
and " took to himself the principal merit of this
" performance." However this may be, it is clear
that the civilians had ceased to be the sole authorities ; the times were indeed changed since the
question of the Spanish Ambassador's conduct had
been referred by Elizabeth's Government to the
exclusive judgment of the civilians, Albericus
Gentilis and Francis Hotman, and since " the
Doctors of the Civil Law " in Knightrider Street
had been consulted *en bloc* as to contraband of war
in the reign of Charles the First. Mansfield's
" predilection " brought him, in 1770, under the
lash of Junius : " you have made it your study to
" introduce into the court where you preside

[1] " Law and Custom of the Sea," Vol. II. p. 307.

" maxims of jurisprudence unknown to English-
" men ; the Roman code, the law of nations, the
" opinions of foreign civilians are your perpetual
" theme." [1] Other instances of the breadth of
the Lord Chief Justice's outlook may incidentally
be mentioned because, as we have already surmised,
it must in time have helped to level the barriers
that had once separated the lawyers at Doctors'
Commons from the rest of the legal profession.
Both he and Lord Chancellor Camden sought instruction from the former upon nice questions involving testamentary law [2] and in 1782 Lord
Mansfield brought the civilians, Dr. Wynne and
Dr. Scott, into the King's Bench in order that he
might be assisted by their arguments upon the
validity of ransom-bills given at sea ; following
therein, it is true, a precedent set by Lord Chief
Justice Lee some thirty years previously. [3] We may
add that this procedure was followed as late as the
year 1845, when the case of *Regina* v. *Serva* (also
known as *The Felicidade*) involving a question of
criminal jurisdiction upon the high seas, was re-
argued by Admiralty lawyers from Doctors'
Commons before thirteen of the judges in the hall
of Serjeant's Inn, after it had come before the Court
for Crown Cases Reserved in the ordinary course at
Westminster. [4] It is difficult to say now what elements of inconvenience and even invidiousness may
have attached themselves to this arrangement, but

[1] Letter No. xli.
[2] Dr. J. Phillimore, " Dedication to Lee's Reports," p. xiv.
[3] For the names of these cases, *vide supra*, p. 62.
[4] *Times*, Nov. 17 and Dec. 4, 1845.

if such there were, they were clearly to be traced to the continued detachment of the College of Advocates.

Employment as a diplomatic envoy, for which, as we have seen, the civilian and canonist had once been eminently marked out, forsook them after the seventeenth century. The eighteenth saw the rise of the Diplomatic Service in the modern sense. Sir Leoline Jenkins was abroad " on the King's service " in 1673, when, owing to the resignation of the Duke of York as Lord High Admiral in consequence of the Test Act, the office of Admiralty Court Judge, which Jenkins held, became vacant : we gather this from the record of his re-appointment, with Wiseman to act as his deputy in his absence.[1] He is again abroad in 1676 at the Congress of Nymwegen : but this appears to be very nearly the last instance of a foreign mission undertaken by a member of Doctors' Commons. At home the civilians still had occasionally a share in treaty-making : Sir John Cooke, Dean of the Arches in Anne's reign, was one of the Commissioners for the Treaty of Union with Scotland, and the doctors helped in the framing of the Treaty of Utrecht in 1713.

The High Court of Admiralty remained, as yet, in the exclusive possession of the civilians, and in virtue of it they enjoyed, late in the eighteenth century, what Professor Maitland has called " a short St. Martin's summer." Between whiles, in

[1] S.P. Dom. June 23, 1673.

the middle of that century, we shall find the procedure of the Admiralty Court employed at great
length about such matters of naval discipline as the
due correction of a master mariner for not striking
his topsail in the presence of a King's ship : though
in fairness it should be added that the real offence
which this formal charge covered was the more
important delinquency, at the period of the Seven
Years' War, of not assisting the press-gang.[1] When
at length, as Maitland puts it, " the British Fleet
came to the civilians' rescue," by providing prize-
cases for adjudication in the Admiralty Court it
happened that there was a great judge there :
and the structure of maritime international law
that Lord Stowell built up during the nine-and-
twenty years he sat in that Court is in modern
times the civilians' " chief contribution to the
jurisprudence of the world." [2]

The great increase in shipping in the nineteenth
century gave to the Admiralty Court a new importance as a tribunal dealing with technical questions of seamanship : the coming of the steam-ship
in the 'forties provided it with a plentiful crop of
collision cases. Its jurisdiction was enlarged in
1840 and again in 1861. But all this had nothing
to do with the Civil Law or with the professors
thereof as such. On the ecclesiastical side the
civilians still kept the testamentary and matri-

[1] " Cases and Opinions," 1758–1774. Burrell's Admiralty
Reports, p. 367.
[2] Maitland, " Canon Law in England," p. 94. As to Lord
Stowell's judicial work see the " Life," by E. S. Roscoe (1916).

monial business of the country at Doctors'
Commons until 1857, and its retention there was
not for its good. Dickens, writing in 1849, did
not leave it doubtful that in his opinion the " lazy
old nook near St. Paul's Churchyard " might well
have ceased to exercise those functions a considerable time before it did. In 1857, however, power
was given by Parliament to the civilians to sell
their real and personal estate and surrender their
charter, upon which surrender " the said Corpora-
" tion shall be dissolved and shall cease to exist for
" all purposes whatsoever " ;[1] and thus encouraged,
the doctors at last put an end to their corporate
existence. It is said that thereupon the rooks,
which some held to embody the spirits of departed
civilians, forthwith forsook the trees in the college
garden. In the following year the right of audience
in the Court of Admiralty, the advocates' last
preserve of importance, was thrown open to the
ordinary Bar.

The association of the doctors of law practising
in the Ecclesiastical and Admiralty Courts, whose
college figures as Doctors' Commons in the annals
of London for more than three centuries thus
passed away for ever. It was launched as an in-
formal corporation at a time when the Roman
Civil Law was making its highest bid for influence
and adoption in this country—a period which
coincides and is not unconnected with the
" enlightened absolutism " [2] of the House of Tudor ;

[1] 20 & 21 Vict. cap. 77, ss. 116, 117.
[2] Busch, " England under the Tudors," I. pp. 291-304.

and perhaps it never quite forgot the circumstances
of its incubation. At any rate these, no less than
its exotic learning, would have sufficed to save it
from ever becoming a popular institution ; but it
was guilty in addition of the fault of living too long.
Men who lag superfluous upon any stage are apt
to dim the fame they deservedly won in their prime;
and so it is also with bodies aggregate. The name
of Doctors' Commons, whence came for the service
of the State a succession of ambassadors, and more
than one jurist with a European reputation,
acquired during the nineteenth century associa-
tions that probably now link in most minds solely
with David Copperfield's articles of clerkship and
the matrimonial misadventure of the elder Mr.
Weller. But if it outlived by many years its
raison d'être it had once upon a time owned a valid
one. The civilians' " contribution to the jurisprudence of the world," made in the shape of that
fabric of Prize Law which Lord Stowell's judgments
fashioned during the Napoleonic Wars, is not quite
their sole title to remembrance. Long before that
they had been concerned, not unsuccessfully, with
the foundation and the building up of a common law
of nations in maritime and mercantile matters.
We are told in Wynne's " Life of Sir Leoline
Jenkins " that " even those who presided in the
" Seats of foreign Judicatures in some cases applied
" to him to know how the like point had been ruled
" in the Admiralty here, and his Sentences were
" often exemplified and obtained as Presidents

there."[1] And, indeed, during its long existence the College of Advocates had given corporate expression in England to that scholarly fraternity with the jurists of other nations which it is not even now undesirable to foster.

[1] *Op. cit.* Vol. I., p. xiii.

INDEX

113